PARANORMAL UNWRAPPED

SHANNON SYLVIA

AND

KATIE BOYD

Schiffer Publishing Ltd®

4880 Lower Valley Road • Atglen, PA 19310

Other Schiffer Books By The Author:

Rhode Island's Spooky Ghosts and Creepy Legends
978-0-7643-3388-0 $14.99

Werewolves: Myth, Mystery, and Magick
978-0-7643-3907-3 $16.99

Witches and Witchcraft in the 21st Century
978-0-7643-3613-3 $14.99

Haunted Closets, True Tales of the Boogeyman
978-0-7643-3474-0 $14.99

Devils and Demonology: In the 21st Century
978-0-7643-3195-4 $14.99

Ghost Quest in New Hampshire
978-0-7643-2886-2 $14.95

Published by Schiffer Publishing, Ltd.
4880 Lower Valley Road
Atglen, PA 19310
Phone: (610) 593-1777; Fax: (610) 593-2002
Email: Info@schifferbooks.com

For the largest selection of fine reference books on this and related subjects, please visit our website at
www.schifferbooks.com
We are always looking for people to write books on new and related subjects. If you have an idea for a book, please contact us at proposals@schifferbooks.com

This book may be purchased from the publisher.
Please try your bookstore first.
You may write for a free catalog.

Schiffer Books are available at special discounts for bulk purchases for sales promotions or premiums. Special editions, including personalized covers, corporate imprints, and excerpts can be created in large quantities for special needs. For more information contact the publisher.

In Europe, Schiffer books are distributed by
Bushwood Books
6 Marksbury Ave.
Kew Gardens
Surrey TW9 4JF England
Phone: 44 (0) 20 8392 8585
Fax: 44 (0) 20 8392 9876
Email: info@bushwoodbooks.co.uk
Website: www.bushwoodbooks.co.uk

Designed by RoS
Type set in Marigold/Trebuchet MS

ISBN: 978-0-7643-4125-0
Printed in The United States of America   Ouija is a registered trademark by Parker Brothers

Shannon's cousin Tressa.

DEDICATION

We would like to dedicate this book to Shannon's cousin, Tressa Collins Odegard, who fought one of the hardest battles a person could fight: Multiple Sclerosis. Tressa shared the same passion for the supernatural as Shannon and she inspired her to live life to the fullest while still here. Sadly, Tressa passed away during the writing of this book. The memory of her beautiful life will always live on.

Shannon's Acknowledgments

I would like to thank my mentor, Katie Boyd, for asking me to co-author this book with her. It's an enormous honor to work with such a great mentor, inspiration, and friend. I also want to thank my husband, Jeff, for bearing with all the late 3 a.m. curfews on investigation nights and for falling in love with the paranormal and all it has to offer as I did. Thank you to my pal and co-inventor, Mitch Silverstein, for sharing ideas and opinions.

Katie's Acknowledgments

Thank you to Shannon for saying yes to co-writing this book with me; you are such an inspiration to many, including myself. You are part of my family, and together, we sure do have a lot to say!

A Special thank you to Psychic Medium Beckah Boyd for such wonderful support while writing this book. A big thanks to everyone who works their butts off in the paranormal every day helping clients; you are appreciated!

CONTENTS

INTRODUCTION

In today's society, the word "paranormal" has become a household name, with new television shows popping up daily on the networks and book store shelves packed with titles on the subject. Paranormal groups are being formed and springing up in every town and city around the world, trying to reach out to those clients who need help, and to collect the evidence of the unexplained realm. What is it that fascinates us so that we want to climb up into dark attics, hike across unknown trails deep into the woods, and call out to unseen forces? Could it be the excitement that flows through our veins or the quest to find the answers to those nagging paranormal questions? Perhaps it is a mix of both.

For many who become involved in the paranormal, it is because of personal experiences or traumatic events that have occurred. It was this way for both Shannon and me. Our goal for writing this guide is to educate, expose, and unwrap the truth behind the world of paranormal. So:

- Follow us into the hardship life of becoming a ghost hunter, the price one pays when suddenly reaching the paranormal ladder, and the criticism each of us encounters.
- Find out about new technologies ghost hunters are utilizing, as well as the best equipment to use during investigations.
- Learn the truth behind orbs and how to tell the difference between dust particulars, lint, and light abstraction photographs.
- Discover the best ways to collect EVPs (electric voice phenomena) and the quality computer programs to use when working with them.
- Learn every step of the way about how to trademark and copyright your evidence and a paranormal group name – as well as what can happen if you choose not to.
- Get insight into cryptids and other supernatural creatures like the Chupacabra, Bigfoot, and the Mothman.
- Let's find out together if aliens are, in fact, real and what the signs are if someone has been abducted.
- We shall explore the issues of television shows, examining the hard facts, and go behind the scenes to see whether this TV medium is harmful or a hindrance to the paranormal research community.
- Learn about the world of demonology and why it has become such a popular subject in the paranormal field.

Together, Shannon and I will take you through the paranormal world we live in every day. Nothing is off limits and no subject is left untouched. You are about to see the *Paranormal Unwrapped*!

"It is wonderful that five thousand years
have now elapsed since the creation of the world,
and still it is undecided whether or not
there has ever been an instance of the spirit of any person
appearing after death.
All argument is against it; but all belief is for it."

~James Boswell
The Life of Samuel Johnson 1791

PART I

world of a Ghost Hunter

"The oldest and strongest emotion of mankind is fear,
and the oldest and strongest kind of fear is fear of the unknown."

~H. P. Lovecraft

The Making of
a Ghost Hunter

In today's society, the words "ghost hunter" are known in almost every household. More and more individuals are fascinated with the subjects of spirits and demons. People are looking for the truth, for answers; and because of this drive, they sometimes find themselves on the path to becoming a "ghost hunter," or as we call ourselves in the paranormal field, paranormal investigators.

Anyone can become a paranormal investigator because there is no such "legit" label as a *certified investigator* – but understand that if you do make your way into the field, it is not all fun and games. The paranormal is not a nine-to-five type job; there are long hours sitting during an investigation to collect evidence. Reviewing the evidence can also be time consuming and can take time away from friends and family. However, working in the paranormal can be very rewarding: helping clients, and other paranormal groups, and even giving lectures on the subject to help educate those who may have the interest.

Those of us already in the field of the paranormal all have reasons as to why we've become involved, but interested folks should be honest with themselves and understand that this work does not come with a paycheck at the end of the week. The cost of equipment comes from a paranormal group's own pockets, and even though many groups have a *donate* button on their websites, most viewing individuals never take the time out to press that button to help the group out with travel costs or even a new supply of batteries. Yet, these paranormal groups still travel to locations around the world every day, turning no one away who may need the help. We commend each and every paranormal investigator because it's not the money that drives them; it's the drive to help others.

What Makes Up
a Paranormal Investigator?

Patience is a big trait; if an individual thinks that by going to a location, or into a client's home, the evidence will just be waiting there (without any work) ...well, think again. Patience in this field is very important. You may need to spend time watching the DVR (digital video recorder) or quad cam monitors, which could take a few hours to days. Researching the history of a property or previous owners can cause an investigation team to run into dead ends, with them spending endless time traveling to libraries, town halls, and other locations to collect information. All this takes time, and sometimes, lots of extra patience, not to mention expenses out of one's own pocket, to accomplish the tasks.

Determination is another quality of an investigator – striving to find the answers to those paranormal issues. Helping the client find a solution to an issue even when it is not "paranormal" in nature is another top priority for investigators and others who work in paranormal fields. This could be anything, such as directing the client to an electrician or even helping the client find the right type of sleep laboratory in their area. One example scenario involved investigators having to recommend to a client the hiring of an electrician because faulty wiring was causing such high EMFs (electromagnetic fields) that many people in a building were hallucinating.

Each paranormal investigator brings varied qualities to the field; this is what makes us different from each other, yet still places us all on the same path – helping the client and finding those answers to the questions each of us are asking.

All too often, ghost hunters are telling clients that their homes are haunted and that other individuals need to be brought in, or worse, they begin a blessing, sage a home, or engage in the use of holy water, or other religious relics. This may happen even before any evidence is captured, simply relying on the client's word and the fear that is causing them to feel uncomfortable in their homes. This is not only damaging to the homeowner and the family involved, it's damaging to the team's credibility when the family still needs relief from the problems they assumed were solved by the team earlier.

Follow up is crucial to a client who is awaiting a response on whether or not evidence was obtained. A report stating any evidence of false positives or high EMFs, as well as detailing any EVPs, photos, or personal experiences should be given to the client so they can be apprised of the outcome of the investigation and any other information pertinent to the case. Many a time has a paranormal team investigated a home, only to never speak to the client again. All that time and energy wasted, only to leave a client still with questions that need to be answered or not knowing what to do to feel more comfortable in their own home.

Shannon's Personal Story

RAGGEDY ANN

My story goes back to when I was a toddler. I ran up to my mother in tears and completely terrified, saying that my Raggedy Ann doll made a bad face at me. I know this sounds completely preposterous, but at the time, I believed it. From then on, I can recount numerous occasions when heavy footsteps would come up the stairs from the basement and my mother would rush my brother and me to the couch so we could read from the Bible until the footsteps went away. For me, this was a part of life – something I assumed was normal and everyone else was doing, too.

THE CROSS

When I was around four years old, I was with my parents at the church late at night while they practiced their songs with the prayer group. My parents, even my brother and I, were the Sunday morning music entertainment and my stage fright began at three when I sang "Mary had a Little Lamb" in front of my church on a regular basis. My brother and I would roam free around the church pews trying to pass the time, reading the booklets strewn about, picking up bingo chips off the basement floor, or hiding behind the old statues in the balcony.

One night, I remember being on my tip-toes looking through the church's stained-glass window outside and seeing a glowing white cross up in the sky. I ran to my mother telling her what I saw, and to this day, she admits she had the very same vision in a dream the night before.

This was not the last I saw of the cross. When I was a few years older, during a sleepless night, I gazed out my bedroom window and saw the same white glowing cross in the sky. To this day, I do not know why, but it has always reminded me that I am being looked after by a higher power.

Being a Roman-Catholic ghost hunter has been a conflict for many years, not only for me, but my family, yet I will never forget what my roots are and how I was brought up. The sightings of the crosses are not the only religious phenomena that have occurred in my lifetime so far; there were many more to come. Many things I choose to keep private from the public but sharing the story of the crosses was the first step for me to express my Christianity and my faith, which keeps me strong while I continue my studies and research. People who know me well know this is one of my traits.

Shannon's Raggedy Ann doll, which terrified her at a very young age by making "bad faces" at her.

MORE CHILDHOOD MEMORIES

The memories of all the hauntings that occurred in my childhood home are endless. I remember many priests from our local Catholic church coming to perform blessings on our house, even the pool. I used to joke around about all the holy water we had. Some of the priests were Father Bianco, Father Pirello, Father Maxfield, and Father Jack. World renowned miraculous healer, Father Ralph D'Iorio, was also a prominent figure in our family's lives for many years. I remember while he was living in Spain and teaching at an all-girls school, eleven young students were my pen pals, writing me often in almost-perfect English. It was very inspiring to me to learn about life in another country from a person my own age.

Things hit a head in my late teenage years, when my mother insisted I relocate my bedroom to the basement, in order to have more room. Half of me was elated to have the extra space I desperately needed; the other half dreaded spending every night in the same place from where the footsteps generated. I proceeded with the move downstairs, and the sleep disorder from which I suffered every single night began to worsen. As if things weren't stressful enough at home, I suffered a great deal of fear from a stalker named Patrick S. (now deceased). Between the police and priests making visits to the house, there was never any calm in my teenage years.

Growing up in "Monsterland" and next to "Blood Town" all in the same vicinity, the Bel Air Heights kids always knew about the creepy neighborhood we lived in, though it did not wreak of dark abandoned houses or consist of hook-nosed neighbors. The neighborhood was pleasant with little crime, and everyone knew everyone's business.

Father Ralph D'Irio courtesy of rdohealingministries.com

I liked my neighborhood. We had a killer garden, a great pool, and my mother allowed me to paint absolutely anything I wanted on my bedroom walls, including an eight-foot mermaid and the Pyramid of Giza. When all my friends came over, they would autograph my wall in black ink or glow in the dark paint.

I had a normal childhood. The hauntings and the stalker are things I kept from my friends in high school; I was too embarrassed to talk about it. Not even my closest friends had any idea – I feared everyone would doubt me and think negatively of the situation, as back then, ghost hunting was frowned upon as something crazy people would do.

Unfortunately, I did have to tell one person; it was my boyfriend of the time – "Jack" we'll call him. We were together through much of high school, and at times, things got so out of control at the house, I would have to muster the strength to tell him what was happening. I'm not quite sure if he really did ever believe me. To this day, one of the scariest days of my life was the day I finally had to tell Jack what was happening around the house as I had no one else to turn to.

One evening, in 1992, my mother left me alone in the house while she went out with some friends. I never minded my alone time; I stayed upstairs watching television for quite some time, until I began to tire around 9:30 p.m. On my descent to the dreaded basement-bedroom, I heard a loud crash coming from below me. Upon walking in, I noticed a porcelain clown face, that had been anchored to the wall, had fallen off and broken into several pieces onto the ceramic-tiled floor. The clown face was part of a set that I had displayed for many years on that very same wall. While I was sweeping the pieces and dust into a pan, I heard footsteps on the floor above my head – heeled footsteps all the way across the kitchen floor – so I darted upstairs to greet my mother, only to find the kitchen area completely pitch dark. I began to worry at this point that something was happening and I was terrified.

I walked back downstairs to my room to wait patiently for my mother to return. As I went back to the part of room where the face had just fallen off the wall, I could hear the voices. I was hearing them on many occasions, but this instance was memorable. They were both male and female and I could not fully make out what they were saying; however, one thing was clear and audible – the name "Shannon." The voices became so loud I was propelled to open the door leading outside, thinking it was a person or group of people on the other side of the door. There was nobody there.

Now panic began to set in and I ran to my bed, pulled the covers and pillows over my head and began to say the rosary. Within about a half hour, my mother returned for the night. I ran upstairs to tell her what had happened and I was given this advice: "Why don't you sleep upstairs for the night?" Well, that didn't make me feel any better. I laid in my own bed trying to sleep after an hour of solid sobbing when the voices began again. I was exhausted, scared, and desperate to talk to someone, but it was around 2:30 a.m. Calling Jack's house and waking his parents was not going to happen. I so badly wanted to talk to him.

That's when the phone rang; and again, panic set in. I answered the phone hesitantly and heard, "Hello?" It was Jack! I kept asking over and over again, "Who is this? Who is this?" because I thought it was the devil calling me! There was just no way in my mind I could conceptualize how someone was calling me at the same time I was desperately thinking about them.

Jack was a bit startled as to why I was crying and hysterical, so I explained the chain of events that happened earlier in the evening. I then asked him why he'd called me at such a late time, and his reply was, "I woke up and felt something was wrong – like I needed to call you for some reason."

Shannon attending Catholic school; faith was always important to her family and they prayed regularly for the phenomena in the home to stop.

My mother allowed me to stay home from school the next day because my eyes and face were so puffy beyond recognition and I'd had no sleep the night before. That night was never spoken about again in the house, and all I could do was plan the days when soon I would be out of the house and into a warm, loving home with no spirit activity whatsoever.

I did find that day, four years later, moving into a beautiful loft located in a renovated 135-year-old school house. It was now a warm and loving atmosphere, but within a few days, the spirit activity resumed. The hauntings at the former Pierce Street School were much different and felt much lighter than the hauntings I experienced on Bel Air Heights.

Ghost Hunting and TV

It took me until 2005 to call a ghost-hunting group in my area that I'd found on the Internet. I had no idea that the ghost hunter who was to head up my investigation was from the television program *Ghost Hunters*. They were a humble bunch; some were TAPS (The Atlantic Paranormal Society) trainees and others were from an affiliate team. The night was long; many EVPs were discovered and we even had a fork fly into a sink causing us females to scream our hearts out from being startled. A second investigation was requested from the leader of the group, and shortly after, I joined the team. After a few training classes, my first-ever investigation with an actual team was Leominster City Hall, in the town where I reside. There, I heard my first disembodied voice of a woman coming from a century-old safe located on the second floor of the massive building. I was elated to finally be doing what I've always wanted to do since I was young – ghost hunting.

In January of 2007, Paranormal State filmed an episode called "Schoolhouse Haunting" in my home. I answered an email from David Schrader stating that a new team with state-of-the-art equipment was seeking cases out of Pennsylvania State University. I emailed details about my haunting and the episode was born.

For several days, the crew filmed at the former school house, researched, and even got in touch with a psychic I'd spoken to long ago in my home. During the taping, they asked me to play for them some of the EVPs I'd collected from my home, as well as those captured by other teams in the past. One by one, EVPs were played; some sounding like a little girl trying to communicate with us were included. I was pleased with the instances that occurred during filming: Light bulbs being unscrewed and heavy breathing was heard by the investigators. An odd appearance by a woman named Katie who used to live in the building happened, thanks to our UPS driver, whose wife was her best friend. Because of editing, the show came out in a very different way than we expected, but the experience of having an investigation for the length of time provided was fruitful.

In 2008, I was cast as one of six paranormal investigators of Ghost Hunters International and was flown around the world to hunt for ghosts for SyFy channel. I was elated to get the phone call late on a Tuesday night to be asked to join the cast, but even more surprised that I was to leave in two days. The journey on the road took us through Scotland, Italy, England, Germany, Romania, Slovakia, Budapest, Prague, and Wales. I stayed with the cast for a year, until I departed before a six-week long trip to New Zealand in order to be present for my new business' grand opening. My attorney was able to relieve me of my contractual duties with the production company in August of 2009.

TODAY...

Since 2008, one of my favorite jobs has been to be employed as a professional speaker for college students at universities across the country, as well as to appear at conventions and conferences. I speak on many subjects, such as paranormal evidence, new inventions and high-tech equipment in the field, and world's greatest paranormal photography through the years. I enjoy public speaking; there's nothing better than talking passionately about something I love and having people interested in hearing about it!

My free time is spent researching. I am currently researching Ouija boards and participating in private investigations with my home team (Earthbound Phantom Paranormal Research Group headed up by David Manch), as well as consulting with Robert Murch of Boston, Massachusetts, who is the world's leading Ouija board expert. I am fascinated with the history and simplicity of the board that so many call a "board game."

Katie's Personal Story

During the writing of my book Haunted Closets: True Tales of the Boogeyman, I wrote many pages about my own personal haunting and how it tore my family apart. Like many, reliving the terrifying experience is not an easy one. While writing that particular book, and the chapter on my family, I received news that my father had passed away. Both of my parents are now gone from the world of the living, but I know they are watching over me in spirit.

Many paranormal investigators of today try to contact me to get directions to the famous home where I grew up. Many contact the local library in hopes of finding leads to where the house stands. I cannot share such information because my family no longer owns the home. It is now private property.

The House in Goffstown, New Hampshire

This is the house Katie grew up in! After the release of her book Devils & Demonology in the 21st Century, some brave souls have been calling the local library to discover its location. Picture is distorted to ensure the privacy of the new owners.

My story begins in a small town called Goffstown New Hampshire, a place where families knew each other and their children grew up together, went to the same school and the same church. There was nothing extraordinary about the town, not that any of us knew about... not until during the research of the town for my book called *Devils and Demonology in the 21st Century*. The information gave me more than I'd bargained for, but put a lot of questions I had at ease.

During 1972, my father had gotten a promotion at the telephone company and had an opportunity to move his family from Massachusetts to New Hampshire. Without hesitation, we moved and bought a small yellow house on a hill. My father and grandfather rebuilt the home from the inside out, making the home larger and expanding the rooms.

Life seemed like any other day, playing with some toy cars with my brother in his room – he was about three years older then me. Out of the blue, I felt a presence, someone watching us; as I looked up and towards the doorway, there stood a large ash-colored individual. There were no details such as hair, clothes, and so on. As any child at the age of four would do, I screamed at the top of my lungs. Blinded with fear, I ran for the doorway and into the hallway, right into my mother who was running towards my brother's room. Fire Face was what I called this entity and I can still see those images in my mind today – images I will never forget.

From that point on, life was never the same for my family or for me. A few years passed with small, odd occurrences, such as lights turning on and off, odd smells like fire burning, or burned hair. My mother felt it would be a good idea to trade rooms with my brother; his room was larger than mine, and I guess a girl needs more space to grow.

The room never felt "right." Every night, my mother would make sure the closet door was shut nice and tight. For some unknown reason, each night, at the same time, the closet door would open and the sound of footsteps would come closer and closer to my bed. Covers were always over my head when I went to bed at night; only on brave occasions would I pull the covers off my head, hoping to get a glimpse of who or what was scaring me. There would be times when I could hear breathing coming closer to me as I lay shaking under my covers; sometimes the bed would press down as if someone was sitting next to me. My parents were very private people and very well known in the community and our local church; our torment would never be told to our close friends or our neighbors.

The issue seemed to get worse and worse as time went by. Our family cat and dog would growl and run away if near my bedroom...and my family started changing moods. My mother would enter my bedroom – she was happy until she stepped that foot across the doorway and into my room. But once inside my room, she became violent (not physically at me), but out of nowhere, suddenly, she would start ripping all my posters off my wall. None of this would make any sense until later on in my life.

While no one was home except me, I would hear my name being called in my father's voice; thinking he had come home, I would run downstairs and into the kitchen. There would be silence, and in fact, my father was not home – no one was. My family was an active one, skiing in the winter and playing golf during the summer, and once we all stepped foot off the property, it was like a huge weight was lifted from our shoulders and our laughter came back. Once we traveled back home and our feet were back on the property, the feelings of being oppressed would come back; the feeling of dread would be back.

My brother started to stay over friends' houses; my father began a strange obsession of collecting colonial-time period muskets and staying in the basement for long hours making lead ball bullets. He never loaded the weapons with these ball bullets, just sat there making them.

My mother decided we needed some type of help and called on Father B., our local Roman Catholic priest, to come in and bless our home and our property. My family was very active in the church and Father B. was a close family friend. During my childhood and adulthood, we did not have any local paranormal groups that my family could call upon for assistance. I started trying to find my own answers as I grew older at the local town's library, reading anything I could get my hands on from every religion to every occult book. Nothing could answer what was going on. Father B. started coming over several times a month due to the strange activity going on in our home. Nothing worked. A few weeks after the blessings, the house seemed to have less heaviness in the air, but all the activity would eventually rise up ten times worse. Nightmares every night at the exact same time would haunt me while trying to sleep in my bedroom - nightmares of burning bodies, bones, and skulls.

Father B. stopped coming over due to a sudden illness and then he passed away. Fights among my family members broke out daily; my brother became violent towards me, my father became violent towards my mother, and I became a solitary teen hiding in my bedroom. My family came undone, and with Father B. gone, we had no one to turn to for help. My brother and I grew older. He decided to move out to live with some of his friends; my father decided to break free from the house and moved out. I was about sixteen years old at the time. Only my mother and I remained in the house.

The house seemed to stand still for awhile, as if thinking on what steps to take next. Then strange occurrences started to happen outside on our patio. Mind you, my father built this patio when I was really little and nothing out of the ordinary ever had happened. My mother and I woke up in the morning once to the patio covered in toads; then, as you turned your head for a few moments, no evidence of toads could be found. Another time it was covered in snakes; look away for a moment and nothing was there when you looked back. I could understand having a snake or two in one's backyard, but a patio covered with snakes and then them disappearing... It just did not make sense. My mother had a pest exterminator come and check the whole property. Nothing was found - not any evidence of toads, snakes, termites, or spiders.

My mother started to spend more time away from the house, playing golf or visiting her friends more often. I, on the other hand, became more withdrawn from my friends and stayed within my bedroom most of the time. When I became eighteen years old, I broke away from the clutches of the house and moved out on my own. Only my mother remained in the house...alone.

This is not the whole story for that would take up this whole book in itself, but a few years later, my mother passed away. She passed away when she sold the home, my father passed away some years later, and my brother has no contact with me. He wishes not to speak of our life growing up in that home and so it is up to me to share OUR story with others in the hope of helping someone else's family - because I could not help mine at that time.

SOME INTERESTING TOWN HISTORY

There is some strange town history, including the land where my family's house was built and still sits today. During 1810, the population in Goffstown was around 2,000 people. There are many who believe that parts of Goffstown (possibly including the center) were built on unmarked graves and that secret societies were prominent around the late 1800s, such as Knights of Pythias in the 1890s, Granite Lodge in 1887, Independent Order of Good Templars in 1869, Mystery Rebekah Lodge in 1891, and more. Native blood was spilled upon the soil of Goffstown when the town was built. Strange fires starting on their own burned the villagers' homes. There was a high murder rate and many suicides. (Goffstown High School is still known by some individuals to be called "Suicide High.") During the early 1970s, Goffstown's Father B. drove out a group of satanic worshipers dwelling in the woods behind an area between Goffstown High School and a private catholic school. I wholeheartedly believe the soil where this town stands today is tainted – and so do many others who still live there.

For many, my personal story does "hit" close to home; I too searched for answers as they did, but found those answers only later in life. My own experiences made my "will" stronger; it made my soul want to fight for those who could not fight alone. Now, they no longer have to do so.

Certifications and Titles

"Education is always great. People should expand their thoughts, theories, and even beliefs concerning subjects of the unexplained. As for certifications, they are pointless and mean nothing to the real world. If I wanted to be an expert or grab a fake PhD off the net I could, but in reality, it's a waste of time and money. It's a scam."

~Tonya Hacker
Paranormal Investigator

Certifications

This was a fun chapter to write because it is such a controversial subject, and Katie and I are no strangers to controversy. A few years ago, individuals began cashing in on the "Certification" process and it's caught on like wildfire. Now, we see individuals completely new to the ghost hunting realm, Googling everything there is to know about ghost hunting. Most individuals come across some form of a "Ghost Hunting Certification Course" while on the Internet and end up spending up to $175 on a certificate that indeed makes them a bonafide ghost hunter.

What is wrong with this picture?

This is looked at in the same manner as employers not accepting some online degree diploma as a legitimate education. It is not legitimate. In this field of metaphysical studies, no matter how much our predecessors tried to prove there were such things as ghosts, it has not been proven yet. It cannot be referred to as a "science." No one has definitively proven there is a life after death.

Plumbers, hair stylists, lawyers, doctors, etc., can be licensed because there are regulations and actual state laws passed controlling how things are done in order to protect the safety of consumers. But we have to ask, what about the ghost hunters? No laws. No regulations. No license. So who is conducting these certifications? Other ghost hunters are – unlicensed, unregulated, and simply passing on their knowledge of ghost hunting to individuals for a fee.

Several years ago, a friend gifted me with the two Dr. Dave Oester Paranormal Investigator courses. After reading through the courses, I took the certification tests. I passed, but have never felt the need to refer to myself as certified, though some may argue I am certifiable. Nonetheless, I learned some practical information from those two courses. Did the certification set me apart or make me superior to anyone? No, of course not. That said, my take on certification is probably different than most. I think the quest for certification comes out of a thirst for knowledge more than a desire to achieve status. As an example, if someone takes a course on how to use ghost-hunting tools and is awarded certification for successful completion of that course, I don't see anything wrong with that. Given the fact that none of us are experts in the paranormal, some will question the certifiers' credentials. But I think that is rather elitist considering these same people who criticize certification, revere others who hold so called parapsychology degrees. Chances are that neither certification, nor the parapsychology degree, will be all that impressive to the person who holds an MBA from Harvard. So if someone wants to learn more about their chosen field, in this case the paranormal, I say they should go for it. And if they are proud that they have learned something, I see nothing wrong with them boasting about their achievement.

~Janice Oberding
Author, radio personality, and paranormal investigator

Paranormal investigating is like a cake: There are many ingredients in the finished product. We may have the hypothesis, the equipment, the vehicles to carry out the work (our bodies), the location, the techniques used during the investigation itself, and the follow-up. Decorate the "cake" with possible use of psychics and new age practices, such as divination, pendulums, or tarot cards.

What one is going to find is that some cakes taste better than others! Every team will have its rules, regulations, to-do lists, affiliations, and individuals they prefer to work with. All of these factors, and the thousands of different practices, patterns, and routines for ghost hunting, are what makes us all unique in the field.

The problem with certification is that newly certificate-christened individuals will be adhering to one set of techniques set by an individual who deems him/herself an expert. However, paying a fee for a course or seminar is not a necessity when joining a reputable team. Experience will be looked at by any team, of course, but a good team will look for things such as photography skills, private investigating backgrounds, and computer and video technician abilities to make a solid team of individuals with a broad skill base. Certifications are not necessary, nor will a homeowner expect the investigator to be certified before stepping foot in the door. Anyone can print a certificate; anyone can also feign a college diploma. However, one will be faced with the biggest test of his or her life without having the basic skills down pat for ghost hunting.

This book is going to give you, the investigator, all the ins and outs – no certificate required.

Upon researching, it was amazing how many individual websites offered online or seminar certification. One online "Home Study Course" offered to coach individuals through their first three investigations, virtually. They would be given a test, and upon passing the test, voila! They were certified ghost hunters.

Another method was the flat rate fee for the afternoon, one such group charging $75 for certification classes. Each individual received a lunch, a beverage, and a manual. If time allowed, the individual would have a chance to go on an investigation with the paranormal team. (IF TIME ALLOWED?) This group also told certification wannabes, that if they wanted to learn how the ghost hunters did their investigations on television, then their course was the BEST one to take. Ummmm, really?

The only difference between Ghost Hunting (101) classes and "certification" courses is the certificate itself. Take a ghost-hunting class recommended to you by others you know or by reputable places online. Attending conferences, special investigations open to the public, college lectures, and expos are other great ways to learn techniques from peers in the field who have been investigating a long time and see the ever-changing new pieces of equipment being used today.

There are many teams offering FREE ghost-hunting seminars. If you have access to these courses, by all means get yourself there and soak in the knowledge – enjoy the free hot chocolate, if you're lucky. Be aware, as mentioned before, that you are only seeing one point of view or one team's point of view. If there are questions, ask away. That is why you and the trainers are there.

In today's world of the paranormal, there are so many resources and sites where you can learn some of the techniques and information regarding how to conduct an investigation or even how to start one's very own group. Also, check out the paranormal radio shows on the Internet which give the listener much-needed education and advice on varied subjects. Katie does a radio show called Ghost Quest Radio (airing Monday nights at 8 p.m. EST at www.tenacityradio.com) that covers educational subjects for the paranormal investigator or even the beginner.

Titles

The President of the United States does not refer to himself as *World Renowned*. Neither does the Queen of England. When is the last time you heard an Academy Awards winner refer to himself (or herself) as *World Renowned*? You won't, because it is beyond ridiculous to do so. People who refer to themselves as *World Renowned* have allowed their egos to override their common sense. Everyone knows they're full of it; rather than impress, they've made themselves laughable. And #1 Ghost Hunter, now that sounds like something a ten-year-old kid might boast to friends. I'm #1 potato bug squashier, and I'm #1 king of the hill, and oh yeah, I'm #1 ghost hunter, too! Apparently, *Top Dog Titles* are important to a lot of people. Look at the magazine that annually proclaims who the sexiest man and woman alive are. Like every adult in the world has posed before their cameras and they have made their selections based on the resulting billions of photos. That's hype, but not hype in overdrive like calling oneself *World Renowned* or *#1Ghost Hunter*.

~Janice Oberding
Author, radio personality and paranormal investigator

Each of us, at one time or another surfing the Internet, has seen the above-quoted words – whether on a person's social website page or on their own website naming someone the "world's number one paranormal investigator" or "world's renowned ghost hunter." Who is giving these titles out and how does the person earn that function? Is there a secret vote which none of us know about, that suddenly gives an individual these titles? Is it to gain more notice or opportunities for the individual?

Most of us who are in the field of paranormal already know the answer, and it's a very risky step if you ask most people. Anyone can give themselves a title; whether it is legit can be questionable. As example, there was a conference where a fellow investigator proudly displayed a large poster announcing that her radio show was voted America's number one paranormal radio show. But, by whom? There is no such title. This woman's name was not on the Billboard Top 100, nor had she sold platinum records. Unknowing passersby or paranormal fans see the poster and assume she has a radio show that is number one somewhere out in the world. This does not bolster respect for fellow investigators. It is not because one investigator is jealous of another, but those involved know the individual is lying to the public.

Unfortunately, this can do more harm than good. Another example is of a man who calls himself "America's Best Ghost Hunter" in advertisements, banners, and on his website. Yet this same individual is infamous for not returning emails and phone calls, and tends to work more on television opportunities then helping people on non-paying cases.

A recent poll was conducted on the social network Facebook showing that ninety percent of people polled believe that those who were "titled" were not credible. Since there is no accrediting institution that can make actual paranormal by-laws, the question becomes: Who can call themselves by a particular title? An individual in the Midwest calls himself an investigator who was "Voted Best in the Country" on his personal and social media websites. This concerning issue then affects the homeowner who is not educated on who's who in the paranormal and who might take a title as gospel. The titled individual could mislead people into thinking they really did ask a prestigious paranormal investigator to help them with their haunting issue.

Is there any benefit to having a title? If having a title makes an individual seem more experienced for financial or physical gain, there would be nothing anyone could do about it. There are no laws broken, but perhaps a few egos are stroked. Our dear friend Steven LaChance, author/radio personality and investigator, had this to say on the subject:

> I think people who call themselves *World Renowned #1 Ghost Hunter* are not only ridiculous in this action, but are also irresponsible and in fact making a fraudulent statement. There are no right and wrong answers to what we are doing. To give the public at large the perception that you are somehow the "expert" is not only misleading, but a lie. There are no experts. I think you can have a knowledge base of experiences to draw from, but that is something that is completely different from labeling yourself #1. Once you put a ranking on yourself like some kind of horse in a race, it gives the impression that everyone else is below you in some way and that is just simply pure fraud where this type of research and investigation is involved. I have seen investigators who have been working for no more than a year do some amazing work who would and sometimes are completely overlooked because of ego statements such as this, when in truth, the majority of those people who make a statement like this are generally doing the same thing all of the time and are never thinking outside of the box. At this point, I would say even if there was such a thing as *World Renowned*, who gives a bleep, because it only means they have sold out and are not actually doing anything of any substance anymore anyway. Most of the time people like this are the "wolves in sheep's clothing" looking for no more than a fast buck and a bit of cheap fame.

Genuine titles in the paranormal *do* exist. However, these are in order for individuals to distinguish specific jobs, training, or interests that an enthusiast may have. Here we shall explain a few of the genuine titles and just what these roles entail.

✓ PARANORMAL INVESTIGATORS (Ghost Hunters)

These individuals investigate locations that are reported to be haunted by spirits. Typically, a paranormal team will attempt to collect evidence claimed to be supportive of paranormal activity, often utilizing a variety of electronic equipment, such as: the EMF (electromagnetic field) meter; digital thermometer; handheld and static digital video cameras, such as thermo graphic (or infrared) and night vision; digital audio recorder; and computers. Traditional techniques, such as conducting interviews and researching the history of a site are also employed.

While many groups claim to utilize scientific methods in their search for the paranormal, there is no ONE standard method for the gathering of empirical evidence established for this pseudoscience – which is why, in our opinion, it will remain a "soft science" for a good time yet. Another reason is that all the evidence is subjective; for instance, when collecting EVPs there are some that are clear and when played for a group, all hearing understand exactly what the EVP is saying. However, those are few and far between; more often we come to see evidence that can be easily interpreted multiple ways, and there in is the rub. We are extremely excited, though, as many scientists in the field of quantum physics are heading towards establishing life after death. There is even now a study being conducted by The University of California on the subject of the afterlife. In fact, the University was granted a $5 million dollars from The Templeton Foundation for this particular study. To read more about it, there was a great article done by Kathleen Miles of *The Huffington Post*. Here is the Internet address to the full article. http://www.huffingtonpost.com/2012/08/02/uc-riverside-afterlife-the-immortality-project_n_1734603.html.

Lead Investigator

When referring to members of a paranormal team, it is common to have a lead investigator who is in charge. This person's job is to decide to proceed with a case at a certain location, dictate which team members will serve what functions on the investigation, and eventually, deliver any evidence the team has collectively gathered to the client. Any team decisions as to who to hire, fire, or train will be conducted by the lead investigator, and, at times, the founder of the group.

Clergy Person

This is a person from any denomination who may be involved in paranormal or in severe cases, such as a call for blessing or an exorcism. Clergy will also be called in to give spiritual counsel, if needed. Home blessings, blessings over individuals, or actual exorcism rites may be conducted by a member of the clergy when called. Typically, the clergy member is recommended by the paranormal team; however, if the client is more comfortable with their own spiritual leader, then we feel it is important that the group go with who the client is familiar with as it will keep them relaxed and open.

EVP Specialist

This is an individual who specializes only in the study and collection of EVP (electronic voice phenomena). The individual has been trained in audio recording under pristine conditions and has been properly trained in the analyzing of recordings in order to properly detect EVPs.

Shannon filming on location in Gettysburg, Pennsylvania, which is considered a veritable paranormal playground!

Demonologist

This is an individual who studies demonic entities and spirits from every culture around the globe, through ancient texts to biblical literature. Most individuals are trained in the study of religions and how each religion works. They have knowledge of tools and how they may be used in rituals, as well as dealings with cultural entities. (Each demonologist works and is trained differently, so make sure to do research on the individual and their background if you plan to work with one.)

Exorcist

This is an individual who is believed to be able to cast out or banish entities, such as spirits, the devil, or cultural entities, from a person, place, or object. An exorcist is properly trained in each of these areas, so please do not take on such a task without the training or knowledge an exorcist would have.

Occultist

This is an individual who studies and trains in a variety of mystical traditions.

Psychic

An umbrella term for people who can feel, see, hear, taste, or smell things that are not available to physical five senses. A medium can be psychic, but a psychic may not be a medium. Oftentimes, psychics used within the paranormal have retrocognition (see into the past) and empathic abilities (able to sense other people's emotions or tap into the emotional energy of the area being investigated). Psychics (not mediums) within the paranormal are often given the label of "sensitive."

Medium

This is an individual who can either hear or see the dead. Some sensitives have potential to become mediums and most often will "feel" the spirits, but this does not make them a medium. The abilities must be refined and focused with a capacity for clear communication.

Forming a Solid Paranormal Team

This process could take a day or many years to complete. Most groups usually start out with two or three individuals, some wanting to just experience or encounter a spirit or some other form of paranormal activity. Most form a group to help those who are having or have had a traumatic experience with the paranormal. Others want to document and collect data, which someday could prove the existence of spirits or even other types of entities or supernatural creatures. Each paranormal investigator has his or her reasons as to why their group was formed. Do not be too surprised if some members decide to leave within a few months of joining the group. This is a common occurrence because individuals do not realize the work and time that is put into paranormal investigations and the "down time" each group goes through before, during, and after a case. Being a paranormal investigator is not all fun and games. It takes away from friends and family; it takes dedication and time.

There are more and more groups being formed with each passing day. One of the reasons is because of the coverage of the subject in the media and due to all the paranormal television shows which air on a daily basis.

Some groups now have a rule set in place for all new recruits: There must be a background check before joining the team. Yes, this is a great step to take for the group, but sometimes we've discovered that a background check does not always show us who that "bad" apple in the bunch is. Do the research on the individual! Ask the questions! Has the person been with another paranormal group before; if so, how long? Why did the individual decide to leave the prior group? How does the individual represent themselves and is it in a professional manner? We are not suggesting that one does not know what to look for in a new member or what questions to ask, but we all have seen many paranormal groups fall apart right in the beginning stages. Have a team meeting and decide what the team needs in a crew member, such as a medical or psychology background. The more varied the types of individuals in a group, the better benefit for YOU and the team.

There will be those certain individuals who want to join a paranormal group to see themselves on television or the particular group's name in the public lime light. Be aware of this and make sure the individual wants to join the group for all the right reasons and not because one group's name is more known than another. If an interested candidate starts "name dropping," make sure the individual is just not name collecting. This means going from one group to another, working with one group for a period of time and then leaving it for another that has made a name for themselves in the entertainment world and in the paranormal community. This is usually a major turn off for most paranormal groups, and in a polite way, an individual will be rejected from joining the team.

Creating a Dream Team

Each team's dynamics are so different from one another, but without rules and regulations from an institute, it's up to the individual team to make everything flow smoothly from start to finish. There needs to be a strong leader who has many years of experience in the field of paranormal investigating. This is vital, as many new members are going to come and go, and training and consistency will be a key to the team's success. The leader must be well-rounded with audio and video skills, coupled with the technical skills needed to acquire and use the equipment correctly. A leader must train, or assign someone else to train, the new members and bring them up to date on the team's rules and regulations, as well as standards the team will go by when they enter an investigation together. The leader must be willing to go to bat for everyone he or she represents and to negotiate any differences within the team. Always make sure to show respect and integrity to any and all individuals. It does not matter if the leader is a male or female, as both sexes in the paranormal are an asset in investigating. In this case, the team leader must also treat both sexes with equality and not play "favorites" to any particular gender or race.

An asset to the lead investigator is having a case manager. A case manager's role is to record information leading to a possible haunting, such as name, address, and pertinent information on the haunting being experienced. The case manager will then notify the team members of the information learned during the interview process. At the end of this book, you will find a sample interview sheet that many teams use as a guideline when interviewing a client for the first time. Many questions need to be asked, such as medication use and any drug or alcohol abuse. It's important to know these details before going in, as many medications and drugs can lead to hallucinations and cause the symptoms the client may feel are spirit related.

Once the case manager and lead investigator decide whether or not the team will move forward with the case, the date and time will be chosen and the investigation process will begin. Some teams will have their case manager actually go as far as to conduct a walk-through at the residence or business. Another interview will be conducted in order to compare notes to see if any inconsistencies arise from the client's story, and base readings will be done around the home or business. The notes are entered into an online database so all investigators can log in, read the case notes, and comment on them. This is where the team gets all the information needed to proceed. Not everyone has the ability to have a fancy online database; however, a group email situation will suffice so every member is notified and using the "reply all" feature will keep everyone happy.

There is no limit to how many investigators should be on a team. It has been proven that if a team has a little "too many" investigators on its roster, it would not be a terrible thing, since not every investigator will sign on to every investigation at every location. This can be problematic if a team consists of only three to five people. Depending on what the team's radius for travel will be, a team assignment is up to the lead investigator. There will be members who simply cannot travel as far as others in order to participate. Time management will also be an issue for some members. Some work weekends or nights and may not be able to attend. Individual time and work schedules should be made known to the lead investigator prior to being recruited for the team.

To be fair to an individual, allow a certain amount of people on a case and set a limit of investigators allowed, depending on the size of the structure. For instance, a three-bedroom, single-level ranch house may only need a team of three to five people, whereas a three-level Victorian with four baths and five bedrooms, parlors, dining rooms, and a haunted basement may require a dozen investigators. It's best to post how many investigators are needed in each specific case, so once the quota is filled with volunteers, it can be capped off. It's better to have more than enough investigators to volunteer than not enough requiring the case to be rescheduled, which does happen often.

It is wise for a lead investigator who is interviewing for a potential team member to ask what the person's occupation is and about former occupations. Any skills that may be an asset to the team are widely welcomed. Some of these skills may include private investigator, photographer, audio/radio technician, electrician, and even a psychic or medium. Any experience with these fields or talents in related fields will broaden the chance that the prospective member will be accepted on the team.

In some cases, however, this may not be true. Paranormal teams may accept members based on their passion for the pseudo-science alone and will not mind training them to the level where they can investigate with the rest of the team quickly. This does happen often and there is no reason this should be shunned, as long as the newbie is adequately trained and does not claim all their learning experience comes from watching television shows. (Yes, this happens!) If you would like more information about having a psychic medium on your team or about working with such individuals, we do have a whole chapter about the subject coming up.

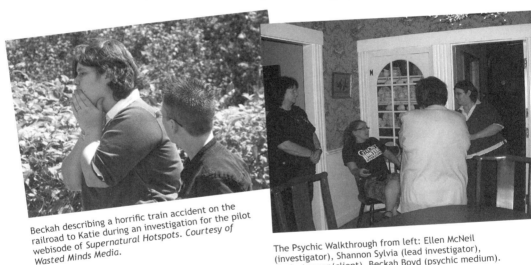

Beckah describing a horrific train accident on the railroad to Katie during an investigation for the pilot webisode of *Supernatural Hotspots. Courtesy of Wasted Minds Media.*

The Psychic Walkthrough from left: Ellen McNeil (investigator), Shannon Sylvia (lead investigator), Gayle (owner/client), Beckah Boyd (psychic medium).

Working with Psychics

Both Shannon and I will share our stories, thoughts, and ideas on this subject. Most know that I (Katie) work closely with a wonderful psychic medium named Beckah Boyd who has also worked alongside Shannon and many paranormal groups around the world. Some paranormal groups only go into an investigation using the scientific methods, which is fine, and that works great for a lot of groups. My own group, Ghost Quest, works with both scientific and spiritual methods by using a psychic medium.

Never base a case solely on what a psychic is sharing or picking up on psychically, but rather use the psychic as a tool and to verify the information about the case. Psychics are a great resource to tap into if an investigator has questions or needs assistance with helping a spirit cross over (helping a spirit or guiding a spirit to the other side), or at times, to give that "eviction" notice (forcing a negative spirit to cross over) to the spirit. Having a psychic on the team is a beneficial factor because most are what we call "fog horns" and will, in some cases, cause a spirit to communicate through the equipment the investigator is using at that time. Yes, spirits do communicate to us even when a psychic is not present during the investigation or collecting the evidence on a case.

There are still many groups and investigators who will not allow a psychic on the team or use one to help the client or the spirit. There are no rules that state any group has to use a psychic, but for me and others, we would rather be safe and not miss an important piece of information that a psychic could provide.

Now please understand that there are those psychics who ARE questionable, just like in any profession; unfortunately, one bad apple can make people standoffish about using a psychic during an investigation or seeking help on a case. This is such a sad situation for those legitimate sensitives, psychics, and mediums. We all have seen those individuals who read a book or listen to a radio show and suddenly announce to the paranormal community or to the public that they are "psychic" now. These are the same individuals who write asking why or how can one tell if "they" brought a spirit home with them from an investigation. Again and again we preach about get the training or education before calling oneself something an individual might not truly be.

Some teams will choose to have a psychic, sensitive, or medium as a part-time or permanent fixture on the team. Most of us have learned throughout the years that this has been a tremendous asset to teams. On many occasions we have witnessed a psychic conversing with a spirit, answering our questions and simply giving us information that was impossible to know. On another occasion, we chose to work with two different psychics on two separate occasions at the same location. The second psychic basically told us the same thing the first psychic revealed leaving us awestruck. A "sensitive" will be able to inform a team about any feelings that come across whether it be a spirit trying to make contact or information read about a location. It is always fun later doing research on the information a psychic has given and finding out everything was entirely correct.

Here is a great method a lot of paranormal investigators use when working with a psychic: Have the psychic meet at the team leader's home and do not reveal any information about the case. Drive to the location and allow the psychic to roam around the building or residence. Get to work taking notes and using physical equipment at the same time, running audio and video recorders. Unlike teams on television shows that promote shying away from psychics on investigations, we have learned to have great respect for the reputable psychics that we all have personally worked with, and the client is always very happy that they were present and contributing information.

Team Rules

Of course, every paranormal team needs ground rules – it only makes sense to have some uniformity and installation of ethics within a team before entering a client's home or business. The last thing one wants to do on an investigation is look unprofessional in front of your new client or your teammates because everything is discombobulated. Many years ago, I (Shannon) received an email from a client who's home my team just investigated, stating how unprofessional some of the investigators had been in his home. During a client interview I was conducting, a female on my team was spotted sitting on a couch with her leg up on the furniture. Later on that night, she was also noted chewing gum during an EVP session and the client felt the urge to write me on how the team could have presented themselves in a more professional manner.

It has been a long time since I have seen these problems arise on an investigation, thanks to some simple ground rules that I have learned throughout the years from various teams and investigators. Below is a list with a description on each rule.

1. Use common sense

Open your eyes, ears, mouth, and nose. If members of your team, or you, personally feel a dangerous situation, by all means, leave. This goes for physical danger in a location, dealing with an aggressive client, or someone under the influence of drugs or alcohol. Listen carefully to the details a client is relating during the interview on the phone, during the screening, and in person during the investigation. Important details the client is trying to relay will not have to be repeated if one pays attention.

Watch the words that come out of your mouth, and what is said in front of the client or to the team members on the investigation. I cannot begin to explain how big of a problem this is in the paranormal field. Completely erase any curse words from your vocabulary during the investigation and watch your manners. Do not release any private information about yourself to the client or your team members during the investigation. Do not do anything inappropriate – if you wouldn't do it on a job interview, don't do it before, during, or after an investigation.

As for using your nose, if you smell any out of the ordinary scents that were not present earlier during the day, by all means speak up! You may be experiencing paranormal phenomena such as smelling flowers, perfume, or even baked goods. Do not keep this information to yourself, because chances are, someone else on your team may have smelled or experienced the same thing.

2. Never be alone

Make sure no team member is alone during the investigation. This is for safety purposes, in case a team member is injured, trapped, falls, or becomes ill. Additionally, in case something paranormal does occur, there will be two individuals witnessing the event. Very often when I am with a group or another individual, there are times we will separate and will go into another room by ourselves. If this is the case, then notify a crew member of your intentions and always have two forms of communication on hand such as a cell phone and a two-way radio.

3. Uncomfortable feeling

This may be due to illness, fatigue, environmental surroundings, such as mold or asbestos, or plain old fear. Do not finish the investigation if a guest or crew member is not feeling healthy. Leave and do not be afraid to speak up. No one wants to investigate with someone who is miserable or having uncomfortable feelings. If you suspect a harmful environment, such as mold, asbestos, lead paint, etc., notify your team leader immediately! This is a very serious situation and could be harmful if one stays in the environment for long periods of time.

4. Alcohol and drugs

Using any type of drugs or alcohol before or during an investigation is absolutely out of the question. If any team member is suspected of drug or alcohol abuse, it is recommended that the team leader take some form of action in removing the individual immediately from the team, client, or area. Refrain from smoking during the investigation and be courteous if one does smoke during down time/break time on an investigation; smoke in designated areas. Be aware that smoke can cause false positives in photographs very easily so be aware of these issues.

5. Trespassing

There are many people across the country who investigate graveyards or outside places, often late at night. But in most areas it is in fact illegal to trespass into graveyards after dusk hours. Time and time again, we hear of paranormal groups or individuals jumping the cemeteries fences. This is not acceptable! Pay attention to the cemetery signs or rules; contact the local Parks and Recreational Department for permission to conduct an investigation after dusk. Notify the local police and let them know who gave your group permission. If a location has been abandoned, do not break the law by entering onto the property to investigate. There have been cases of amateur ghost hunters going to jail, even being killed by trespassing in unsafe areas. It is possible, in some cases, to get permission from unlikely locations in order to conduct research. Simply ask the owner or contact the authorities to explain about the group's purpose and why your group would like to go into an unauthorized area. Listen, what does one have to lose by asking permission? The most you will hear is *no* or sometimes, surprisingly, *yes*.

6. Respect the spirits

Respect the spirits as you would the living. Remember, in many situations the spirit may not even know he or she has passed and could still be dealing with the trauma caused by the death.

Do not barge into a room and provoke a spirit by yelling at them or swearing. This is not a joke and we are dealing with someone's dead relative. Did we suddenly forget that these individuals were once people with feelings and could be in a state of confusion or in need of help? It is also not *kosher* to behave erratically in front of a client who is scared and wants answers regarding what may be haunting their home. Be professional and courteous; ask questions that you would like to be asked if you were in the spirit's ghostly shoes!

7. Extreme cases

If you or your group is not professionally trained in these types of investigations, DO NOT take on the case. In today's paranormal field, there are many highly qualified individuals who deal with extreme cases on a daily basis. Katie and I have seen the poop hit the fan on many occasions when a group feels they can take such a case on for themselves. If an investigator or a team leader feels this is or could be an aggressive case that borders something sinister, leave it to the professionals. Do not play a role such as a demonologist and scare the home owner any more than they already are. On a weekly basis I am told horror stories, one that depicts an inexperienced team having misused holy water or provoked activity to the point the family was terrified. After the team has left, the family is faced with more trouble than they started with and are confused as to who to call next or what to do.

Please use common sense and do not delve into something you are not trained to do because it seems "cool" or gives a person a form of bragging rights for your team's resume. Both Katie and I have gotten emails or phone calls from paranormal groups who went into a client's home and realized this was a type of case that was not in their area of training, but had the smarts to call us to find the right kind of help.

8. Charging for services

Most paranormal groups do not charge a client for an investigation, but do accept donations to offset travel expenses. Charging for paranormal investigations or asking homeowners to pay you for your services is absurd for obvious reasons. We are all here to conduct research and possibly help a homeowner or a business learn about their haunting. You are not here to profit off someone else's misfortunes. The client is allowing the investigator or group to come into their home or place of business to conduct the investigation and collect the evidence. It is a fair trade. Many paranormal websites have a donate button for clients or people to help out with the cost of running the website and buying the equipment. For the investigator, cost for every piece of equipment, gas for the vehicles, and even the batteries do come out of pocket, or in some cases, groups do have a set amount for dues, which each team member pays monthly. Many professionals, such as Katie who has been in the paranormal field for over twenty years, does not even charge clients. Yet, time after time, we see paranormal groups or professionals charging a client and getting money for a client reaching out for help. Clients are reaching out to us and some are so desperate for answers that yes, they will pay for a solution, but what happens when the solutions do not work? Is there a money-back guarantee for the client?

9. No whispering

Do not whisper during an investigation or while collecting EVPs. One of my personal pet peeves is reviewing audio from an investigation, and just when I think there is a Class A EVP... nope; upon further examination, I discover it was an investigator in the room making a comment in a whisper. Use normal talking voices so your associates will know who was talking and not mistake it for the voice of the spirit of Uncle Ralph trying to communicate. This same rule applies for noises you cannot control such as shoes squeaking, the chair a crew member is sitting in, and so on. Acknowledge the noise that was created so others will know when they hear it on their recorders to dismiss it.

10. Smells

Refrain from wearing perfume, cologne, or body spray the day of the investigation. In many cases of paranormal activity, there are scents present that are very important in identifying the issue or haunting.

11. Be objective

Educate the members on the team about the art of debunking and what things and situations might be around that can cause false positives. The last thing one wants to do is place the client on edge with information from someone on the team who assumed a piece of "evidence" was paranormal. The talent for debunking comes with experience for all investigators. The more each of us is aware of our surroundings and what causes certain things to happen, in a particular way, the more professional the investigator or team will appear (and be). Remember, not all cases involve spirits or demonic entities. Do not just assume; interview, investigate, and gather as many solid facts as possible before ever labeling a case.

These are just some of the rules that most of us in the paranormal have adhered to and have worked successfully. There are of course many, many more points we could make, but those points will come out in other chapters of this book. Since there are no set rules and guidelines by any licensing or accredited institutions, ethical guidelines, such as these mentioned, are adopted worldwide.

Paying Investigating Fees

So how much should one expect to pay to investigate a home? Absolutely nothing; however, one may run into the occasional fee to enter a well-known location in order to investigate.

According to national standards, it is not ethical for a paranormal team to collect a fee from a homeowner. Since the field is unregulated, without licenses and permits, no team is deemed any better than any other team. The paranormal is still considered a hobby; therefore, it is not normal for one to expect compensation from a client. It is perfectly acceptable to receive a donation from the client to cover gas and travel expenses, but a fee charged to a client to investigate their home is frowned upon. Now what happens when the client turns the tables and wants to charge the paranormal investigator to do an investigation in the client's home?

There was a situation in Massachusetts, around four years ago. Shannon was asked by a homeowner to investigate his home, free of charge. Her team found amazing evidence both photographic and via EVPs and was given the opportunity to come back a second time. The case was then filmed for a national television program and word began to spread about the hauntings that occurred in the home. Unfortunately, the home changed hands and the new owner began to contact paranormal groups to exploit the home to willing investigators. The team was asked to pay a fee to the new homeowner so it could go towards the restoration of the home. It is an unusual situation because you have here a homeowner offering his primary residence to possible investigators, but at a price. Whether or not the money really goes towards a "restoration fund" no one will know, but people are paying the money to investigate the home that was featured on the popular ghost-hunting show. Paying fees to homeowners to investigate their residence is not common and is not widely accepted.

What is widely common and acceptable to most investigators is paying a fee to investigate a historical, commercial, or public building. When asking permission to investigate such a venue, one needs to keep in mind the costs to keep the building in business and upgraded to code to allow investigators and other visitors to do business with them. Employees will need to be paid in order to chaperone or assist throughout the investigation until everyone is ready to go home. Structures, such as lighthouses and historical locations, depend on tourists and ghost-hunting enthusiasts to keep the business alive and thriving since most of these places do not receive state assistance to stay open. Fort Mifflin, in Pennsylvania, is an example of this kind of venue that depends on investigators to pay a fee to enter so the location can continue upkeep on the land.

There are literally thousands of locations here in the United States available to paranormal investigators free of charge. There is an online resource, The Shadowlands website (www.shadowlands.com) that lists reputed hauntings nationwide, broken down into states and cities. The website can point the individual in the right direction as far as assisting in finding the free location to investigate in the vicinity where you live or plan to visit. Search the Internet because there are many sites out there that have state listings or posts about cool and free places to visit. Check the local bookstores for haunted regional books, which, in some cases, give the reader specific directions to the locations.

Leave the Drama Behind

"The only reason for people talking behind your back is because you are already ahead of them."

~Fannie Flagg
From the movie *Fried Green Tomatoes*, 1991

Touching this subject is like opening a large can of worms, but both Shannon and I agree this book would not be complete without writing about it. Each of us, at some point or another while working in the paranormal field, has found ourselves or a team mate either involved in drama or around dramatic issues. We know many investigators and others who may be having varied kinds of drama in either their personal lives or with regards to the actual paranormal community. When this happens, oftentimes, they will not attend an investigation or they may even take a small break from the work and the team. This is a good call to make and we agree 100% with the resolution. We must remember that if one goes into a client's home or onto a property, we do not want to be carrying our own personal "luggage" into the case. This is a harmful situation for the individual, group, and the client. Spirits and other such entities may turn those issues or dramatic feelings and situations against the investigator – or worse, the client.

Now, what about drama within the group? Of course, that happens – and more often than we would all probably admit. What about drama between groups? Again, happens way too often, and instead of joining forces, we become enemies. How foolish this is and how ridiculous we all must appear to the public. Not really a cool image to show the world, is it? No paranormal group or investigator is better than anyone else; each works differently when in a group or when alone. Since when has it become a competition? If it turns competitive, then each of us has failed.

Unfortunately, whether a person is in the knitting club or chess club, or works as a doctor, or as a paranormal investigator, there is going to be some degree of drama. When there are people of different backgrounds, experience, or education levels, each harboring opinions, at some point, not everyone is going to agree. From case bookings to evidence, it is natural for people to disagree to a certain level. But what level of drama for a team is too much?

When team members voluntarily leave the group or a member has to be fired, there is stress placed on the team. The team leader or founder of the team, must find the source of the problem and quickly deal with the issue. If a team member approaches the team leader, or team leader goes to the members with concerns, the problem should be accomplished diplomatically. Anger and aggression will never solve an issue. The team leader should approach the person involved and do his or her best to resolve the issue properly. If everyone puts their minds to a problem, it can be solved more efficiently.

As mentioned, each member was selected to be on a team for one reason or another, whether it was because of an occupation, education, or experience. Every person has their own role to fill. If one is part of a team that is a "sinking ship," it may be best to retract yourself from the team graciously and move on to find another team that can fulfill the interest. For instance, Joe is a smoker. He frequently smokes cigarettes on investigations. Against the team leader's advice, he takes frequent smoking breaks outside while the others remain inside with the client. What is wrong with this? Not only is the client likely to be upset because the team cannot stay together and appear structured, but Joe is disrespecting the leader's orders and possibly contaminating photographic evidence. If the leader of the team is unaware of Joe's habits of smoking during a case, it is up to someone else to talk to him or her and let them know this certain behavior bothers the members. Correcting the behavior civilly and promptly will relieve stress for the surrounding investigators who have to deal with that individual.

If talking face to face or sending a cordial email to an individual who cannot follow team rules or respect everyone's boundaries on the team is not successful, then by all means, the decision to remove the person must be made. Giving warnings can be a successful way of telling individuals that they need to straighten up or they will be released from the team. Unfortunately, many teams have members leaving in bad faith and the negativity continues to linger no matter how one tries to resolve the issue and go their separate ways.

For some reason, drama seems to be rampant in the field of paranormal in general. Yes, it happens in all areas of life and work as well. We often scratch our heads pondering why an individual we know is a target of a drama attack. Some individuals are just prone to cause drama of some sort in another person's life. People may become jealous of others for how they may be presenting themselves, who a person may be friends with in the paranormal, or who they work with. This is such an unfortunate event because paranormal investigation is supposed to be fun, educational, and professional.

Some degrees of drama are as small as slanderous remarks made on social-site posts to as drastic as involving restraining orders and dodging death threats. Jealousy and competition-fueled aggression is present from many individuals and comes with a cost. It is our hope to outline some of the types of drama and what possible resolutions may be available to bring peace to all the parties involved.

Social media networking sites are awesome to be a part of: Anyone can connect with friends, family, and meet new individuals. This is such a wonderful way to also reconnect with just about everyone – even those who one has not spoken to in years. In my (Shannon) mother's case, she found our maternal family members in Milan, Italy, and felt compelled to pay them a visit over a pasta dinner. There are so many benefits to the social network; for work, play, school, networking with hobby enthusiasts such as yourself, and to find out about cool happenings in a town near you. But with the whirlwind of optimism of finding and being found on the Internet, there are those so-called downsides.

Oh, the drama...is there any other field so drenched in drama? I seriously doubt it. Someone is always ranting, heartbroken, ecstatic, angry, and doing someone else wrong in the paranormal. Sounds like the daytime soaps, doesn't it? The reason for all this drama, in my opinion, is that the paranormal field has become so intensely competitive. While some might deny it, all want recognition and glory and yes dare I say it, a TV show. But there is only so much glory, so much recognition, and so many TV shows to go around. This is where the trouble and the drama begin. Ours is a field in which the learning curve is short, today a newbie tomorrow an expert, scoffing at the views and opinions of others. This is where the trouble and drama really start roaring. To get ahead in name recognition, the formula is always the same: Form a group, get members and an area to rule over. Team shirts and signs on one's vehicle don't hurt either. We're like Hollywood, and like it or not, the paranormal is perceived as a stepping stone to fame and glory and yes, that all important TV show. People who proclaim we're in the paranormal to educate and to find answers are lying through their teeth. Watch us as we take on the paranormal. We're booking engagements. There is no way to get rid of the drama. As long as the paranormal is seen as a springboard to stardom, it will be filled with drama. If you doubt this, just take a look at the entertainment world...and the old black-and-white movies of Hollywood heydays like All about Eve. Muuah...air kiss...muuah...air kiss...Look out for that knife. That's our drama ridden paranormal field.

~Janice Oberding
Author, radio personality, and paranormal investigator

Social Media Sites

"The Internet is both my lifeline and the plastic bag over my head."

~Manisha Thakor
Personal finance expert and author

Did the world have as much drama as it does now before television, email, blogs, and social media networking websites? Do you remember being bullied the old-fashioned way years ago by being teased, pushed, taunted, and ridiculed in person? How many times have each of us taken a look at social site news feeds and read an individual's ploy to call another person "out" or post a blog slandering a certain individual? Who do we believe and do we take the time out to hear both sides of the story or issue? Many do not and jump to the first conclusion about another individual. We are preconceived to think a person is guilty – and without knowing all the facts or even knowing the person being attacked. People suddenly hate him or her because of what someone else has said on the Internet. It may be that this person has never even been met.

If someone does have solid, hard facts, however, that there are illegal actions taking place, it is your right to bring awareness to others. For example, a few years back Shannon posted a blog about an individual who had swindled many people out of thousands of dollars. This was an eye opener for many, but also a horrible experience to endure. This individual claimed to be a psychic medium from the United Kingdom; he claimed to be "famous" by being a part of a western side of the United States. People needed to be educated about this individual's scams. Posting a blog on several social sites brought awareness to the public and to those in the paranormal field. This person took funds in advance for different events, did not pay vendors or people he employed for varied services, and when paid for private consultations, he followed through only when he wanted to, which was infrequent at best. Additionally, the reputations of other psychics were damaged, making them victims of distrust by others in the paranormal. Conclusion as to what came to be of this individual? Sadly, most people did not receive any type of reimbursement of their lost money. Word spread of the issue, and without anyone knowing, the individual just up and left the country. Each of us, at one time or another, will encounter betrayal from an individual or co-worker in the field; this happens everyday to people, and not just those in the paranormal.

If for any reason an individual discovers content posted on a website about themselves, family, or a friend, the first thing that needs to be done is to *not* contribute to the post with your own opinion. Fueling the fire is what the other person wants the attacked individual and everyone else to do. This will get no one anywhere, but will cause upset feelings or anger. People may fall for hearsay, but taking part is more damaging than good. Best is to simply stay out of it – the best way one possibly can.

We do recommend letting the slandered party know what "you" have seen and where, but keeping a professional stand on the matter. Contact the person directly who is posting negative information about another individual, letting them know how bad this makes them or their team look (not to mention their place of employment!) in a simple, communicative manner. Many times, some of us have even had to intervene with two or more individuals who were virtually fighting, asking both parties to see how much damage the attacks were doing to their reputations without even a resolution at the end. Sometimes by intervening, the action will decrease the negativity surrounding the issue. This method is not fool-proof, but by not taking part in the verbal assault, and recommending a cool-down period for all involved might help.

Some social sites (such as Facebook) have a great policy of allowing users to report abuse in blogs, wall posts, and status updates. All one has to do is report the actual comment that is defamatory or abusive with the click of a button, and staff at Facebook will decide if the posts, or the users themselves, will remain in public view. This is especially handy in reporting sex offenders, people using too much profanity, or for those slandering an individual, race, or group of people. In extreme cases, the social site will likely remove the user permanently. Even when a person tries to speak the truth about another individual or about a certain subject matter, "attackers" will swarm at the chance to rip the person up without, again, gaining all the facts. They will turn the tables; suddenly *you* are the one being attacked (for doing what exactly?). Telling the truth... funny. How does that make any sense?

If an individual is constantly seeing negativity and drama actions or comments from another on the social site, try to remove them as a friend or block them altogether. It is illegal to defame or slander a person to the point where it adversely affects their business or standing within a community. Now mind you, this only applies if they are telling untruths, over exaggerating, or stating opinion as being factual. So you cannot go after a client who says they did not care for your services. However, if they lay claims that you stole from them (and you didn't), then it is considered libelous for both the website that is hosting the blog and the writer. Most companies, including social sites and website hosts will aid someone who feels they are being slandered. All you need to do is give the information to them. Keep it pertinent to the situation; they may not need the entire back-story but just the main points and the proof. Give them the site name or user account (if it's a social site), the exact post (or link to the slanderous portion of the site) including time, day and URL – if you can get a screen shot of it, that is even better. Send it to the complaint department or host master for the site. In some cases, the hosting company will remove the user account or website altogether!

Stealing Evidence

Stealing evidence is another major problem in the paranormal: Just about every team has experienced this issue or has been in position where evidence has been used without their permission. Most of the time, this occurs from a former team member who has left the team, taking the evidence with them, and displaying it as their own by showing the evidence without the owner's permission, on a personal website or social media networking site without the proper permission. This is where copyrighting all evidence comes into play and a great way to avoid this issue. It is important to remember that the minute that someone writes a work, draws a picture, snaps a photo, or records an EVP, it has become common law copyright, this means that the person owns and is the originator of this piece of intellectual property. If you are unfamiliar with the term, it refers to any creation of the mind and can be separated into two distinct categories:

Industrial Property – which includes inventions (patents), trademarks, and most things related to business.

Copyright – which covers literary and artistic endeavors including photos, recordings, films, books, drawings, paintings, and sculptures.

The gist of it is if someone is going to use another individual's pictures for any reason, written permission must be secured. This way, if at any point there is a dispute about the use of the picture or any evidence for that matter, the owner will have the written permission from the original creator to show as proof.

For more on what IP (intellectual property) is and to find out if you are covered, you can check out the World Intellectual Property Organization which has a wonderful handbook and pamphlets on understanding how copyright and other related rights work.

If a person grabs the photo as their own, it will open them up to an infringement lawsuit and that can be costly. There are so many gray areas when it comes to copyright! For instance, if I (Katie) write a blog about ghost hunting 101, then Shannon reads it and gets inspired to write one, too, incorporating some, but not all of my ideas and in her own words, well then I can't do anything about it. However, if she decides without my permission to copy my entire work, and has it accepted by a major magazine in which she is amply paid well, that is plagiarism and covered by copyright law. No matter what you are doing, when it comes to evidence, your team name or anything else for that matter, be sure to get informed. A trip to an intellectual property attorney is a great investment to give you a feeling of security. There are a ton of great resources out there to take advantage of, from forums with actual practiced attorneys who monitor and answer your questions to checking out the source at www.copyright.gov (The United States Copyright Office) or the U.S.P.T.O. (United States Patent and Trademark Office) for tons of great information.

We conducted a poll on a social networking site and welcomed our 5,000 virtual friends to vote on this issue. Forty-five percent of those who voted reported having their team's evidence stolen from them by another peer in the paranormal community.

There are some steps to get one's evidence back with a few emails or letters. Contact the person who is posting the evidence as their own in writing. It is very important to have everything in writing! Save a copy of the letter for reference. In the letter or email, simply state the website URL where the evidence is presented. Ask them to cease and desist using your property. It is normal to set a time limit to give the individual adequate time to update a website through a webmaster. One can find a standard cease and desist letter anywhere online just by searching. If you prefer, send it yourself to save the costly attorney fees for having one made up. State in the letter that you want all property removed, sign the letter or email it in your own name. Physical letters are a bit more effective in this case because they can be sent certified, making it easy to know the individual received the letter. The party cannot then claim the letter was not received. If the party refuses to remove the evidence belonging to you or the group (this is rare), it is now time to notify an attorney.

Lying

"When you stretch the truth, watch out for the snapback."

~Bill Copeland

Why on earth does an individual have to boast about themselves to look larger than life? Believe it or not, it happens more often than one might think. Self-inflation is not only a pet peeve for many people, it is almost criminal in some cases. There are millions of television fans who watch paranormal and ghost-hunting television shows, and those individuals absorb everything like a sponge, including every detail of every episode. People grow to adore the personalities on the screen with fierce adoration. Some people may hear others talking about how a certain person is simply not the same off camera as they are on camera. Yes, this may be true on a person-to-person basis, but many believe the personalities on television are "god-like" and they can do no wrong. That is a high standard for the televised individual to uphold, and we have seen how quickly these same individuals can fall off that pedestal.

Many paranormal investigators are not on television, but some do aspire to be – whether or not they are vocal about it. Some individuals start to make up personal name titles or falsify information to make themselves look better to a client or others in the paranormal community. An example we can discuss involved receiving a phone call from another paranormal group. Without doing their homework on just who they were calling, they went on about how wonderful their group was, trying to intimidate through the phone – merely because the two groups were close in location proximity. The caller talked about how great the group was and made it sound "over the top." This is a sad behavior. Why does a group need to try to be something they are not? In fact, this caller was part of a new group and was still in the beginning stages of setting up the group. Unreal! It made an impression, but not a very good one. One does not need to lie to make their group, or themselves, look better than another. All of us in the paranormal work differently and so do paranormal groups. Inflating an individual's ego just creates tension around those who know the person, especially if the information is not true. Falsifying information about one's self makes all of us who work hard every day to help clients, as well as other paranormal groups, look bad.

Other examples include:

- A man in California faked evidence on camera and has been pitching a new television show for years in the hopes it catches someone's eye.
- A Massachusetts man activated a K2 meter (a type of EMF meter) on demand by calling a special phone number stored in his cell phone as "Ghost Phone," leading the team to believe the hits on the meter were legitimate. Upon review of the sent calls list on the cell phone, it was revealed that numerous calls were made to the number in the middle of the investigation, and at the same time the K2 meter hits were recorded. This individual now appears on several paranormal-related television shows as an "expert" and is represented by an "agent."

This kind of lying and fraud is all around us, no matter what state we live in, and we all may know someone like this.

One of the biggest reasons individuals are compelled to fabricate evidence, or their capabilities as a paranormal investigator, is to gain the attention of television producers and/or the general population. In 2007, there were a few dozen Internet radio shows dealing with the paranormal and ghost hunting. This number has shot up to a few thousand in just four years. There is no lack of variety by any means: There are broadcasts for anything from UFOs to psychic call-in shows where readings are conducted on the air for free. A handful of Internet shows, even some television programs, feature investigators who fake evidence in order to gain ratings and popularity amongst those in the community. Unfortunately, when someone is discovered having faked evidence, all hell breaks loose with a show's ratings and reputation. Yet, there are individuals out there who will go to all ends of the earth to be in the public eye, no matter what the consequences – credible or not.

There are also individuals who search other paranormal groups' websites to see what places have been investigated or what media the group has utilized. Some of these individuals will contact the group's sources and steal their ideas or try and make the group's accomplishments their own. We've even seen instances where a co-worker in the paranormal, only just met, will be asked to be a guest at an investigative location, only to find that the information gleaned from this courtesy is used to produce their own Internet video show at that same location at a later time. Suddenly, an email notice arrives inviting the original group to come and watch this Internet video show, making themselves look cool and the ones who had the idea originally.

This happens all the time, but there really is not much that can be done about it, except move on and be the better person. Both authors have broken ground on numerous locations, been the first to discover "virgin territory" never investigated. Then turn around and with a couple of well-placed blogs, a facebook status, or a small bit of media attention, we've had that same place get checked out by a ton of other investigative teams. Yes, we had the original idea to go to this place, but this is not stealing. You cannot steal the idea to investigate a business, home, or piece of land (unless you have an exclusivity contract with the owner to be the only investigative team) and it is great to see other people backing up evidence (or not) that you collected! However, when you are building your name, your new technique, or technology and someone steals it right out from under you, or you find frauds who claim to be the "#1 paranormal investigators" because they want the extra attention they feel that self-given title bestows on them... well just so you know: The truth always comes out. This is again lying to the public and to others in the paranormal field who do not lie to the public, falsify information, or commit fraud. Another social site poll that was conducted in June 2011 and readers voted "Fraud" as the number one flaw in the paranormal today. This covers theft of evidence, theft of funds and ideas, lying, and cheating.

Trademarks and Copyrights

Trademarks are so important in today's world. We all have seen, heard, and experienced horror stories from those individuals who have decided not to take those extra steps and protect their evidence, logo, or group's name. Most do not take the time to double check to see if a name is federally trademarked or copyrighted. This, right off the bat, could save so many people headaches in the long run. It is simple enough to do! If you are naming your group after your city, like Tulsa Paranormal, it would not behoove you to look on the federal level, but rather the state, simply because it is highly unlikely that there will be a Tulsa Paranormal in surrounding states. You will want to register a DBA literally meaning "doing business as" or a state registered trade name. DBA's are cheaper, but do not afford you all of the same rights as a state trade name. Try talking to someone at your Secretary of State, Corporate Division; they can usually point you to exactly what you need. The paper work is simple enough to fill out, and with a check, or credit card, and a few signatures, you will be up and running in no time. However, if you have a common name or one that is not localized, you may want to go all the way with a Federal Trademark. This can cover you across the country and even overseas! To learn more about Federal Trademarking we suggest going to the USPTO website at www.uspto.gov. Oftentimes, they will tell you to get a trademark attorney to fill out the paperwork for you, which can become incredibly expensive, but the USPTO employs their own attorneys who are incredibly helpful if you are stuck on a certain part of the application.

It does not matter if an individual is into the paranormal or a song writer; protect the work that you are putting your blood, sweat, and tears into. This happens in all areas of life – suddenly someone else is making money off your song, book, movie, brand, or name.

It's All in a Name

Many times we have seen paranormal groups try to use another group's name. Psychic medium Beckah Boyd and I (Katie) co-founded Ghost Quest back in 1999. Thank goodness we had decided to trademark this name, but even though we did, some individuals still try to get away with using it. Yes, it is a very cool name, but we did not pay the fees of $325 for others to use this name without our permission. When Beckah and I filed for the trademark name, there were many individuals who tried to contest our process. This happens when others want the name that is being filed for. It was not an issue because the one who can prove that the name was in use for the longest period of time gets the name. We had all the proof ready to show the assigned trademark attorney, and months later, we received the gold-stamped trademark papers.

Steps to Setting Up Your Trademark

1. Go to USPTO.gov and check the TESS database (may also be labeled trademark search). (Research information for varied countries.)
2. If you see your name is taken, look at what it is registered for. Paranormal *is* a form of service listed under the USPTO site.
3. If it so happens that the name is used, then think about changing your own to avoid any possible legal issues in the future. You may also want to think about applying to the Supplemental Register at this point, which is for trademarks that do not meet the requirements of the Principle Register, but are still looking for recognition. Once accepted, it will also allow you to put that glorious ® next to your name. Mind you, much like the state's DBA we talked about earlier, the Supplemental Register offers limited protection. Typically, it is used by people who have already had their mark added to the Principle Register in their own country and not yet done so in the USA.

The United States of America

CERTIFICATE OF REGISTRATION
PRINCIPAL REGISTER

The Mark shown in this certificate has been registered in the United States Patent and Trademark Office to the named registrant.

The records of the United States Patent and Trademark Office show that an application for registration of the Mark shown in this Certificate was filed in the Office; that the application was examined and determined to be in compliance with the requirements of the law and with the regulations prescribed by the Director of the United States Patent and Trademark Office; and that the Applicant is entitled to registration of the Mark under the Trademark Act of 1946, as Amended.

A copy of the Mark and pertinent data from the application are part of this certificate.

To avoid CANCELLATION of the registration, the owner of the registration must submit a declaration of continued use or excusable non-use between the fifth and sixth years after the registration date. *(See next page for more information.) Assuming such a declaration is properly filed, the registration will remain in force for ten (10) years, unless terminated by an order of the Commissioner for Trademarks or a federal court. (See next page for information on maintenance requirements for successive ten-year periods.)*

John Doll

Acting Director of the United States Patent and Trademark Office

Katie's trademark certificate for her paranormal group Ghost Quest

4. If it is available, you want to file for the Principle Registe
   is where all of the "incontestable" marks go). Once it is
   Principle Register, it cannot be contested for five years (the time
   when you must renew your mark); at that time anyone can come
   forward and attempt to claim it, although you at this point have
   provenance with it.
5. Now is the fun part, you've filled out your Initial Principle Registration
   Form (which you can file on-line) and now you get to sit...and wait.
   This process can take months before it goes through completely.
   Be patient!
6. For those who may have to go through the Supplemental Register,
   fear not; once you have built a bigger reputation around the mark
   through extensive use or you've been on the S.R. for five years, you
   will be eligible to petition to have the mark moved to the Principle
   Register.

Now, what happens if an individual has a .com and does not have the
name trademarked? The individual with the .com may contest the trademark
name, but only if the individual has been using the name in question for a
longer time than those contesting it. Once, Beckah was asked to have her
own radio show before she started with the *Psychic Switch* show she does
now. The network owner asked what she wanted her show to be called and
Beckah replied with the name she desired, since for several years, she'd had
a social site by that particular name. Without her consent, the individual
bought the .com and left Beckah speechless (and rather upset) because
she wanted to obtain the .com herself. Now this individual has ownership
over the radio show name because of the .com purchased, and refused to
change it over so Beckah could buy it. After one radio show aired, Beckah
decided to leave the network and then bought the federal trademark of
the name. Beckah cannot use the name for a radio show, but she can use
it for everything else, i.e., books, magazines, social sites, and so on. This
individual can only use the name in radio content and nothing else. So,
because Beckah had use of the name by creating a social site, she was able
to get the trademark for journals, magazines and social media. However,
because this individual owned the .com and established ownership of the
name as a radio show, she will never be able to have one under that name
or file a trademark for such, and it was a hard lesson to learn.

Tips

- When you register a website at a place such as godaddy.com, be sure to
  not only purchase the .com but the .net and .info as well. This shows
  your serious intention towards using the domain and the mark.
- If you find someone already owns that domain name, pay attention to
  the alternatives that show up on the side bar of the website. However
  if that person is within the states surrounding you and doing the same

thing you are, then you may be out of luck and want to try a different name. The whole point is that you don't want people to mistake your group for another with the same name or vice versa.

- Just because you bought the domain name DOES NOT mean you have to set up a website as soon as possible. You can sit on it a little bit.
- Once you buy the domain name, it establishes your common law copyright which gives you a limited amount of protection; this can also be enforced by registering for a state or federal trademark.
- Be sure your name is relevant. Many within the paranormal are into acronyms! If need be go for your initials, but don't call your group "The Great Ghosties" and then name the website Michigan Ghosts.... keep it relevant to your name and content.
- Keep it simple! If your name is super long do NOT try and make that your domain name. For instance Ghost Quest Paranormal Research Society, pretty long name right? So what do we do...we call it Ghost Quest.
- Be aware of cyber squatters. When I (Katie) founded Ghost Quest along with Beckah Boyd, I got to face an interesting challenge as I discovered that someone had bought the name GhostQuest.com. When going to the site, I discovered that it was a parked page and they wanted upwards of $6,000 for it! Unfortunately, because the site is not being used for paranormal or really anything, I cannot demand its release from this company. If you run into this issue, stick an inane word in front of the name such as "the" or "official" in order to make it work.

AUTHOR NOTE: MANY USE WHAT IS CALLED THE "POOR MAN'S COPYRIGHT"; THIS IS WHEN A PERSON SEALS INFORMATION OR A FORM OF A LOGO INTO AN ENVELOPE AND MAILS IT TO THEMSELVES AND NEVER OPENS THE ENVELOPE. THIS CAN PROTECT YOUR PROPERTY, BUT ONLY TO A CERTAIN POINT.

Another time, there was an individual who tried to use our paranormal group's name, Ghost Quest, for their own group's name, never doing any type of search on the Internet or elsewhere. Our lead investigator happened to do a search on our name – always a good habit to keep track of your group's name by randomly searching – and noticed that a website was portraying our name in a less than favorable manner, having pictures posted of the individual with a beer can and half-naked women by the person's side.

We wrote a nice *Cease and Desist Order* for the person to please change the name, for we owned the federal trademark. The individual called us names and said they intended to block our email address and to "go bother someone else." In turn, we wrote to the site company and showed proof of ownership of the name; the site company quickly removed the individual's website. I personally wrote to all the social sites the individual was using to let people know that our trade name was being employed without our permission; again, all pages and sites were quickly taken down.

Now the other disturbing thing was that this individual kept using the name, including for a local cable-access station in the person's hometown. For years, our own paranormal group did a local show as well and happened to stop due to our schedule being rather busy. The odd thing was that for this individual's show, our same color for our group name was used and almost the same logo. We contacted the station and showed again the trademark proof; the show was off the air quickly.

What was unbelievable was that, in the next day or so, I received an invitation to speak on a friend's radio show, and Ghost Quest, and the individual who also was claiming to be the founder of Ghost Quest, was scheduled to appear on this same show. I contacted the radio host and explained the situation and how there had been no permission given to use our group's name. This show host contacted the individual and explained the Ghost Quest name could not be used due to infringement issues. The show host decided to cancel the show and received some rather nasty messages from the individual about there being a verbal contract between them. The show host had no issue having the individual on the show as a guest, but could not use the name Ghost Quest. This did not go over well, so then the threats came about suing the radio show. In return to the threats, the show host stated that this individual was falsifying, impersonating, and infringing. The messages then stopped.

As all of these issues with this particular individual were occurring, I had even gone to the lengths of scanning the trademark papers and putting them on all my social sites to show others who, in fact, owned the name. After this incident, emails started to pour in, stating how this same individual was even stealing other paranormal groups' video evidence and using it as their own under the Ghost Quest name. We then contacted the video site where the individual was posting the videos. It was simple enough; we sent them the link to our trademark in the TESS system and lodged our complaint. They emailed us once for clarification, and within three days, the account was handed over to us. That done, when the account was wiped of videos, we noticed a flag on the account and got in touch with a photographer who had actually made a complaint against this person. Turns out he was also illegally using photos this person had taken! We introduced ourselves to him and let him know the situation; the photographer was more than happy to speak with us and we ended up with a great new contact!

This was a horror situation to go through, weeks and weeks of sending proof to sites and having the individual still keep using our name as theirs. This situation happens to many, but with a little time and proof of ownership, there is much that can be done to stop such an individual. The next step would have to be taking the person to court, but suddenly, the individual decided to join a friend's paranormal group and stopped using the name Ghost Quest. Beckah and I then decided to go onto Shannon's husband's Internet talk show called *Up for Discussion* and share information on trademarks and our personal horror story on the subject, in hopes to help others or answer questions on the subject. You can find that archive at pararocktv.com or listen to the first episode of *Ghost Quest Radio* on tenacityradio.com where we discuss in detail copyright and trademarks.

Ghost Quest Paranormal Research Society
CLIENT INVESTIGATION FORM

DATE:

ZIP CODE:

STATE:

CELL NO.:

NAME:

ADDRESS:

CITY:

PHONE NO.:

EMAIL:

DATE OF BIRTH / AGE

OWNERS/OCCUPANTS NAMES (INCLUDING YOURSELF)	GENDER (M / F)	RELATIONSHIP	

STRUCTURAL INFORMATION

☐ Other

☐ Apartment

☐ Condo

☐ Duplex

BUILDING TYPE:
(CHECK ONE)   Detached Residence

LOT SIZE (SQ.

SQUARE FEET:

DO YOU OWN OR RENT?   BATHROOMS:

NO. OF BEDROOMS:

ADDITIONAL ROOMS & OTHER INFORMATION:

HOW MANY YEARS AND/OR MONTHS HAVE YOU LIVED AT THE LOCATION?

1

Basic Interview

Evaluation Forms

Each paranormal group usually has their own type of forms for a client to fill out prior to an investigation; this can be done by either snail mail or through email. Jack Kenna, who is a paranormal investigator with the group Supernatural, Paranormal, Investigations, Research, Intuitive, Truth Society (S.P.I.R.I.T.S) of New England, writes what we feel to be the best field reports and evaluation forms out there. Most evaluation forms cover the basics such as:

- How long has the activity been going on?
- Has anyone in the household bought any antiques in the past month?

Make sure, first of all, that *your* group has all forms covered, from client investigation agreement forms, client interview forms, evidence and media release forms, the client follow up or after care forms to investigators' investigation report forms. Be creative and think outside of the box when putting together the forms. Ask questions such as:

- What type of television shows does the household watch? (This is important to know because sometimes individuals can unknowingly focus on a subject that has been watched on television and suddenly feel they too have that same issue.)
- Is there any documentation of previous paranormal activity (such as newspapers, books, and so on)?
- Has the home or area ever been checked for types of mold?
- What type of over-the-counter cold medicine does the household use? (Again, these types of questions are very important because some over-the-counter medicine, if taken over the suggested amount, can cause audio and visual hallucinations.)

There are no dumb questions and asking as many questions as possible could help the client and the paranormal group in the end.

When a client contacts the paranormal group, most try to describe what is going on or issues that are arising in that first contact. By having the group send a basic evaluation form to the client to be filled out and returned, the information will identify the serious clients and the non-serious ones. If a client truly needs the help, the form will be sent back to the group ASAP.

As mentioned, most paranormal groups already have their set of forms ready and this is great information for those groups that may be just starting out in the investigation process. Remember to:

- Document everything
- Keep all initial emails or snail mail that the client sends to the paranormal group
- Keep a call log for all clients who call

This is a record for the group to have on hand in case an issue ever arises.

Some paranormal groups also have clients sign a separate form upon their arrival to the destination, which might state that all damages beyond the paranormal group's control will not be the responsibility or liability of the group. This does not mean a group can destroy the client's property, and then, in turn, say it was due to the unseen forces that resided in the client's home. However, strange occurrences like furniture or an object flying across the room or area and smashing against the wall or floor do happen during investigations, or even at the initial client interview. This should not be a liability assigned to the group.

Having all the proper forms for the client looks very professional and gives the client a sense of comfort that the paranormal group is serious about helping. Make sure a media release form is signed by the client; this is so the group is given the permission to display any evidence or pictures on the group's website or through any other sources (books, magazines, interviews, etc.). This is a must do for *all* groups, because if for any reason the papers have not been signed and a group posts evidence or pictures on their websites or other public places, this can cause trouble. It's possible that (because of societal opinions) a client might be fired from a job, or a range of other mishaps. The client could then try to sue the paranormal group, claiming their loss was due to the posting of evidence and so on. Mind you, this type of case might not stand up in court, but it will not shine a good light on the paranormal group, even if it was not the group's fault. Always cross the T's when it comes to clients and investigations; this will only save the group headaches in the end. Also remember that there will be those times when a client does not want any evidence of the investigation posted on the paranormal group's website or used in any way. Make sure in cases like this that there is also a form for both the paranormal group and client to sign; stating all information and evidence which has been collected during the interview and investigation is confidential.

PARANORMAL UNWRAPPED

The iWay invented by Shannon
Sylvia and Mitch Silverstein.

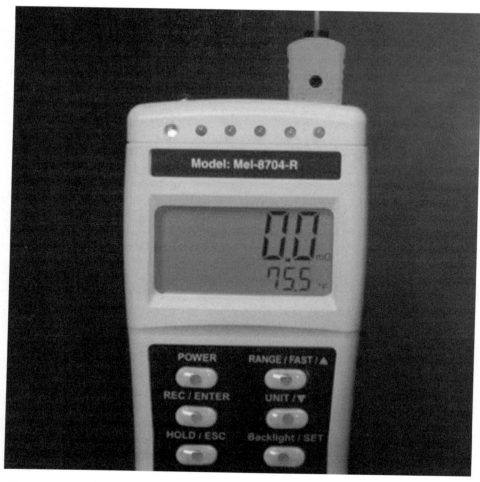

MEL Meter courtesy of ghoststop.com.

Advance Equipment and Research

There are so many pieces of equipment out there for every level of paranormal investigating, and everyday new pieces are being invented for the field. So now, let us move on and talk about the possible upgrades to the equipment collection.

The Mel Meter

This offers simultaneous EMF and temperature readouts at once. The device offers both single axis AC magnetic field measurement and real-time air temperature readings. Basic one-inch K-Type thermocouple is included and it can be used with a variety of commercially available thermocouple probes for extended temperature ranges. Solves the age old paranormal equipment problem of "How do I hold all this stuff?" Use the meter for base readings on investigations in many areas to record temperature and EMF readings in every room or area of a location. Some investigators choose to use EMF readings as possible "responses" from spirits during an EVP session. This can be done by asking the spirit to fluctuate the surrounding temperature to a certain number on the Mel Meter or EMF detector.

Thermal Camera

Originally used by firefighters to detect areas of heat or to search for victims, paranormal investigators have fallen in love with this expensive piece of equipment for ghost hunting. These cameras function by recording the infrared portion of the spectrum. Using infrared radiation, the camera will show colored variations on the screen. Though usually hailed as a must-have for ghost hunters, its hefty price prevents many from owning such a device.

The downfall of this product is that it will record *any* heat signature trace. People leaning on a wall minutes earlier, handprints, footprints, anything from our bodies will be imprinted on an object for a surprisingly long time. Rodents, bats, birds, etc., will make outdoor use unbearable when searching for anomalies. They are very expensive averaging $4,000 and up, depending on the model and features. If the model does not have video output, there is virtually no use to having one. Recording the evidence is pertinent.

DVR (Digital Video Recorder)

First used by banks and stores for security purposes, the now ever-popular DVR system is almost a staple for every ghost-hunting team. Though not required for every ghost hunter to own and operate one, it's an asset to run one on an investigation. The DVR consists of a VCR-looking box that records, can rewind, fast-forward, and save your data onto the built-in hard drive. It connects to a monitor of any size and enables an investigator to view different areas of a haunted location based on how many cameras are connected to the system. The camera angles average from four to eight scenes for viewing throughout an investigation and where you hope to see paranormal activity as it records the session for later viewing.

Full Spectrum Digital Camera

This camera was originally used by various geological researchers and the military for remote sensing as early as the 1950s. It is now also used as a tool for ghost hunters to capture images the human eye cannot see using UV and infrared-light technology. Your average digital camera can detect the visible light spectrum up to around 400nm - 1000nm. When the camera is altered, the capabilities bring the spectrum range anywhere from 350nm to 1200 nm - farther than the eye can see.

Digital and Analog Cameras

Digital cameras are a staple piece of equipment for most paranormal investigators, but understand that digital cameras can be rather sensitive in picking up dust particles, rain, and humidity, which can show up as false "orbs." So before jumping to any conclusion that the picture has an anomaly in it, make sure it is not light reflection or refraction and so on.

Analog cameras are great to have along with the digital camera because an individual cannot tamper with the pictures and the negative picture is a hard copy. (Remember Polaroid cameras? They are analog cameras.) Digital pictures can be manipulated.

EVP Collecting and Programs

One of the easiest ways to gather evidence when investigating is through EVP (Electronic Voice Phenomena). EVP work is simple, inexpensive, and fruitful for the beginner enthusiast. With a little training and a few tips, one can be on their way to collecting evidence of the afterlife. So just who was the individual who started the EVP trend and how long have investigators been at this type of recording?

Who ever thought a photographer would be the first person to attempt recording the voices of the dead? Always interested in psychical research, Attila von Szalay first attempted to use a recorder in 1941 as a way to enhance his current investigative efforts. During that time, the recorder he carried only went 78 rpm which was incredibly slow. It wasn't until fifteen years later, when he began to use a reel-to-reel tape recording apparatus, that he really saw results. Working with Raymond Bayless, a fellow researcher, he conducted a bunch of different experiments. Modifying the recorder as they went, eventually they just created a custom piece with a microphone in a separate insulated cabinet, which connected to the recorder; it also had a speaker which allowed for things to be heard in real time.

Atilla should have been extremely excited by his finds! From initials to well wishes for the holidays, the two researchers decided to write up an article all about their findings and submit it for publication in the well respected American Society for Psychical Research in 1959 almost twenty years after the initial idea hit Attila.

Bayless didn't stop there; he eventually wen on to co-author the book Phone Calls From the Dead in 1979.

We have come a long way since the 1940s in technology, but the theory still remains: Voices of the dead are able to be captured with audio recorders. We have already covered what kind of recorders are recommended in use for communication, but now let's cover what techniques work better and learn how to extract EVPs from the recordings.

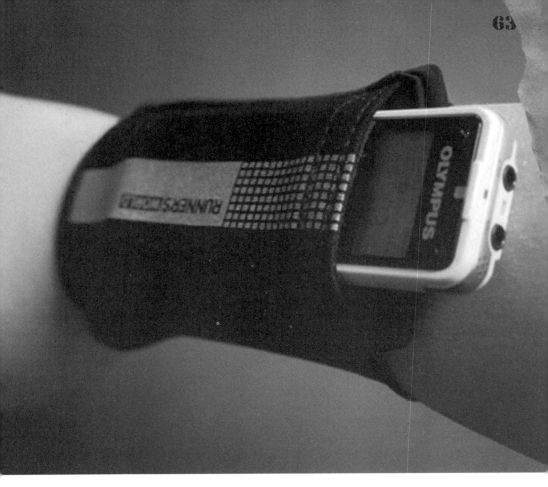

EVP Armband courtesy of ghoststop.com

For starters, there is free software available on the web called Audacity (http://audacity.sourceforge.net/). This allows an individual to queue up the recording and do just about all one will need to do within the free program to extract your EVPs. Simply open the audio file that has been placed into a designated folder, say "EVPs" and allow the file to import into the software. You will see the frequency lines of the file in its entirety. We recommend splitting your audio files up into chunks periodically during recording so the audio file is not too long and complicated to work with later on. Listen to your audio directly from the software in case you need to quarantine a clip that may have EVP on it.

When looking out for EVPs, one must be careful with how the audio is recorded in the first place! Placing the recorder on a steady, quiet platform will give the best results, as well as making sure the room is not contaminated with voices from the investigators and clients. If the team members acknowledge their own noises and voices, it makes for smooth sailing when listening to the audio at a later date. There will be no pondering if something is evidence or not; the individual will know what to eliminate. EVPs can be broken down into a certain class depending on how clear and audible the noise is on the recording.

CLASS A

For an EVP to receive a Class A rating it must be a very clear voice and everyone who listens to the recording agrees on what is being said by the spirit or other such entities. Everyone who hears the voice must come to the same conclusion about what is being said without being told by another investigator. These voices do not need to be amplified or cleared up using a computer sound-editing program but can be clearly heard straight from the recording device. It does not have to be extremely loud but it must be clear. The Class A EVPs are the best voices of the dead captured and are the rarest to record.

CLASS B

A Class B EVP can be understood, and most people agree on what is being said. These EVPs might not be understood by everyone who listens to them and might even sound like the recording is saying something completely different to varied people who listen to the recording. This class of EVP might need to be amplified using a computer and a sound-editing program before being clearly understood. To get a Class B rating, the voice must be fairly clear and easy to determine what most of the words are, when analyzing the voice with your computer. This is the most common class of EVP captured!

CLASS C

The Class C EVP will be the worst quality voices that you can capture. It is nearly impossible to understand what is being said, even with the help of computer enhancement. These EVPs are often just whispers or mumbled words or might even sound robotic. The voice cannot be understood, but the investigator still knows that it is an EVP because no one was talking during the recording session and human-sounding voices can clearly be heard in the background noise.

CLASS R

In order for an EVP to receive a Class R rating, it must have a meaning to it when played in reverse. Some EVPs will have a meaning when played normally and a different meaning when played in reverse. When this happens, it will have two classifications. For example a Class A EVP with a excellent and clear meaning in reverse as well, would be titled a Class A-RA, EVP. This means that it was very clear to understand both forward and in reverse. It cannot have a Class A-RC because this would mean that it could not be understood in reverse which would not be a Class-R EVP. You may have a Class B-RB or a Class A-RB, etc.

When one believes that they have a recording of an EVP, it is best to segregate that section and rename the file with the words the EVP is stating such as "get_out.wav." For easy cataloging and location of the file at a later time, this is the best way to label the work. In some cases, one may find that the background noise of the file is a bit too much and needs to be eliminated. Adjusting the noise option in the software slightly will remove the hiss and crackle of background noise yet keep the original audio intact.

One should always remember to play EVPs backwards! On many occasions we have captured an EVP that sounded perfectly normal played forwards but when reversed we could hear a completely different message. This Class-R phenomenon still bewilders audio experts and investigators alike and it is fascinating to think that a dead spirit is capable of such remarkable ability. In 2006, I captured an EVP of a young man saying "I can't do anything" after I asked if the spirit could do anything to show us he or she was present. After playing it backwards I was amazed to find that the EVP said, "I can't do this!" in the same young man's voice. Both are Class A EVPs.

It's an Orb?

One of the biggest challenges experienced paranormal investigators are faced with, is the inevitable dust-orb evidence photo. Before I (Shannon) had training on the subject of dust orbs, I too assumed that every orb was a bodiless soul floating around the atmosphere luckily finding its way into my photographs. My good friend, Robyn McKinney, taught me long ago about the various types of dust orbs and false-positive photographs that are revealed to us from time to time. In this chapter, we will help you understand what the differences between the various kinds of particle orbs and true orbs are. This chapter is vital to any beginner paranormal investigator as orbs in photographs are so prevalent that the assumption one has caught a true paranormal orb can be easily believed. Here are some examples of orbs that are most common and what they are:

Dust

Dust particles can contain small particles of human skin cells, pet dander, pollen, paper fibers, dirt, and other microscopic particles. Every home, business, and building contains dust, no matter how clean the surfaces may appear. Dust is in the air and we breathe it in every day, only to be filtered through our lungs.

This photo depicts several dust orbs taken in a dark room which can be captured very easily using a camera with flash activated. Take some snapshots in the dark of a clothes dryer with the door open exposing the lint filter. Notice the few "orbs" that may be caught with an individual's digital camera. Now, create this scene very easily by tampering with the lint screen with your hands, moving the dust about, then placing

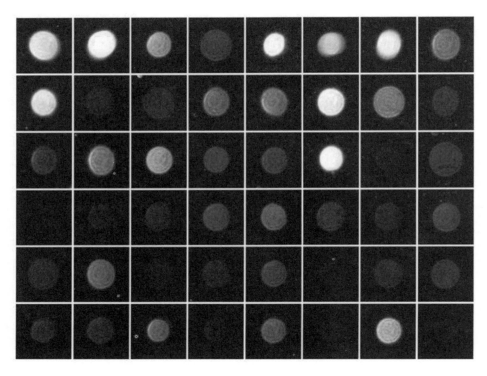

Collage of photographs containing dust from various sources. *Courtesy of midnitewalkers.com.*

the screen back to its original position. Snap some photos in the dark of the area and compare the first photo to the second one and note there are significantly more "orbs" in the second photograph. Upon zooming into the orbs, you will notice they look exactly like most orbs depicted on the Internet and from various paranormal photos shown in books or on television shows. These are not ghosts at all! Just dust, lint, or other debris.

Many people will question as to why the orbs vary in transparency, or why some are darker than others. It is a simple answer; the particle was literally further away from the camera's flash at the time the photo was taken. The brighter the "orb" appears to be, the closer it was in proximity to the flash therefore illuminating the particle with the light reflection. Another reason is that since dust is made up of more than one material, the density of the content can vary therefore appearing darker or lighter on camera than its surrounding areas. As far as various colors in dust orbs, the way the color appears to our eyes or the lens of the camera can be compared to how a rainbow works. The light is refracted thus causing several different colors to

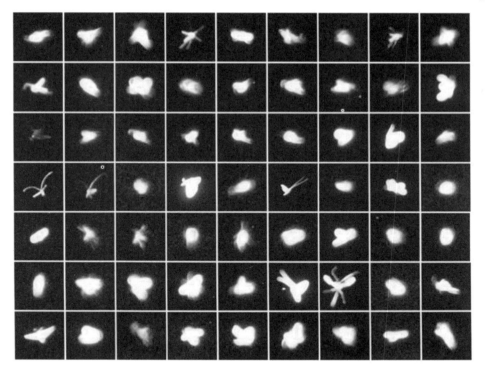

Various photos of bugs in different stages of flight. *Courtesy of midnitewalkers.com*

appear to our eyes depending on the angle one is viewing it from. A colored orb will work in the same way as a light source (flash) is being used and the moving particle (dust) is in motion. Another common mistake is that of a photograph of an insect flying at night. An investigator will swear that there were no bugs around at the time a photo was taken, or even indoors; however, bugs are more common than we all think!

Bugs in different stages of flight are often mistaken for "fairies," "vortexes," or paranormal entities. As with the dust orbs, a bug can also reflect light off its wings and body, causing a motion blur or odd shape to appear on the camera's lens. Antennas, legs, and wings are the most common shapes that will give away an insect's appearance but also their torso and head may or may not be prevalent in photos.

Insects fly very fast in most cases so the person taking the photograph may not even realize it was in the frame. One has to be most careful indoors when flies, mosquitoes, and moths, among other insects, can reside wreaking havoc on photos taken in the dark. I once had a moth the size of a golf ball hit the hand of an investigator next to me and I swear to this day we never saw it coming or going. It was a complete surprise it was even in the house, but it was there alright!

All of these photos and examples are in this book to teach you about false positives on film. In order to prevent mistakes like this from happening, there are things one can do to eliminate the possibility of false positive photos from ever leaving your camera or computer into someone else's hands for an opinion.

When taking digital photos, it is recommended that one use a "slave flash." A slave flash will provide a stronger illumination when the photo is taken, but, most importantly, the flash source will not physically be close in proximity to the lens. With the newer digital cameras being used more often in the paranormal today, the more "false positives" will occur in photographs. Do you remember when you were younger and you saw photos taken with Polaroid instant cameras or with 35mm film? If you do, then you will remember that there were no orbs in the photos. This does not mean there were no spirits around us in the photos, it just means that digital cameras were not used and the flash was positioned in a different place than most of the models of cameras you'll see on the market today. The flash was many inches away from the lens and the cameras were much bigger decades ago. These are actual, technical reasons orbs did not frequently appear in most pictures from "way back when."

Other things that will cause false positives in photographs are camera straps, breath, fog, mist, moisture, smoke, airborne debris and more. Camera straps are extremely common, although one may think it did not make the money shot, it most certainly can get in the way last minute and create what some will call a "vortex"' effect. I always recommend one uses the strap during photo taking so it's around the wrist and not dangling on the side.

With breath outdoors, simple fog can form when the difference between temperature and the dew point is five degrees or less. There is no such thing as a set temperature as to when you'll see your own breath, but depending on the temperature and air pressure, you can certainly experience this phenomena even when it is in the 60s (F). When taking photographs outdoors, one should always hold their breath while taking a photo to eliminate the possibility of the photograph showing fog or mists. Being aware of one's surroundings before compressing the camera's button will save a lot of heartache and headache later on and help contribute to the paranormal field's debunking skills all around. More people need to be a bit more skeptical when shooting photographs. It is extremely rare to actually capture paranormal activity on film using a camera. In all my lifetime I have only witnessed three photographs that I could truly call paranormal.

Interview with Mitch Silverstein

Mitch Silverstein, founder of Nyak Paranormal.

Can you explain for our readers a little bit of yourself and why you became interested in the paranormal?

I have always had an interest in science. It was sparked by my visit to the 1964-65 New York World's Fair where the latest technology and the Space Age were popular themes and a wonder for a six year old. A few years later, *Star Trek* captured my enthusiasm and my career path in the sciences was set. I wasn't quite a science nerd, I had a fairly typical childhood in suburban Long Island, New York, and eventually my interests found me receiving my Associates degree in biology. The sciences of observation led me to my bachelor's degree in Psychology with an emphasis in experimentation. I soon landed my first job out of school in a clinical human genetics laboratory. I got to know chromosomes all too well. For the next twelve years I supervised clinical genetics laboratories doing cytogenetics, biochemistry, molecular biology, and a little chemistry. Then I had the opportunity to utilize my skills in lab operations. I am currently Senior Director of Facilities and Laboratory Operations for a small biotech company in New York. I get to keep things running and also do science!

My son, Kevin, had a keen sense for science, a natural at math too. So it was an interesting leap for us to start doing paranormal investigating, since most of our interests were based on facts. We watched the shows on TV in disbelief – there were no controls; how can we believe them, how can we, as scientists, do it better? So we attended our first event, met some fun people, and began our quest to challenge current theories as Nyack Paranormal. We thought of ways to test equipment, add controls, and actually set up an experiment to locate positions of EVP within a room. Since my son and I were the whole team, we enlisted help from friends with experience and essentially set up an extended team. Our laboratory is the Shanley Hotel, which has proven to provide us with data and with the opportunity to meet amazing people, such as Shannon and Jeff S., the newest team member Stephanie B., and honorary members from all states. We believe you can try anything to find evidence of the paranormal, but we believe even stronger that you must be severely critical of what you find.

What did you want to be when you grew up?

Always wanted to be in science, a scientist. Funny, I went for accounting the first year of college! Then switched to Biology. I eventually did become a scientist and am currently in laboratory operations.

Tell our readers about what you do in the paranormal field.

I consider my efforts research and development (and having fun). I like to collaborate with good people, develop equipment, and techniques that challenge theories and adds control to investigations and experiments.

What is your coolest piece of equipment and why?

My coolest is the quadraphonic recording apparatus we use for experiments that we developed. Doesn't fit in your pocket, but it has interesting implications towards collecting EVP data. Besides iWay, lasers and tripod, and RF detectors, my Secure and Steady Dowsing Rods have provided million-dollar expressions of frustration on people who claim they can dowse!

Do you hold any degrees or certifications?

I have an Bachelor of Arts in Psychology and an Associates of Applied Science in Biology.

What bothers you most about the paranormal field and what can you do to make it better?

Drama is the worst part of the field. It's insane to be so competitive based on really nothing. There is no tangible proof to fight about! I attempt to spread the word that we are all in this to collect data and share the data. Realize this isn't a science, but maintain scientific thought. I want people to remain skeptical but not cynical. Keep an open mind, but scrutinize all data severely. Anything I develop or co-develop will be shared with others in the field. This gives us the best chance toward discovery.

What sets your team apart from other teams?

We strive to develop and conduct experiments with specific goals in mind. We also rely on OTHER teams to provide feedback and experience in these experiments. We develop simple equipment to challenge theories and improve the investigation process.

What equipment in the field does not work whatsoever towards finding paranormal activity and why?

Personally I have *never* used a thermometer for any investigations. Most places investigated are prone to temperature changes and drafts so the thermometer stays home. There is no equipment that can be proven to detects ghosts, most are off-the-shelf items designed for other uses.

What is the equipment you can best recommend to a newbie in the paranormal field to start?

I have three items I would highly recommend (besides your own senses!). Flashlight, if it will be dark; a voice recorder, since a possible EVP seems to be the most common result to an investigation, and a camera to document the site being investigated (layout and personnel), not to capture anything paranormal.

Demonology in the Paranormal

Many question the subject of demonology being associated in any way with the word paranormal or the paranormal community. Being a demonologist for over twenty-two years now, I am on the fence with this debate. True demonic cases are very rare to experience, but the cases that *are* real do have some form of unexplained paranormal activity present, including spontaneous fires, larger objects (like a couch or a kitchen's refrigerator) teleporting to a different area of the home, religious objects appearing desecrated, and odd markings (such as writing or scratches on the victim's body) that disappear within hours of the attack. Of course, this is just naming a few examples in demonic cases.

Some paranormal investigators confuse the signs of a negative spirit haunting with the signs of a demonic haunting. Signs of a negative spirit attack can range from being pushed by an unseen force to having a kitchen chair (out of nowhere) suddenly fly quickly past a client's head. But what, in fact, is demonology, and why has the subject become so popular among paranormal investigators.

Demonology is the study of spirits/demons from biblical texts to all religious cultures and folklore. Now, not all individuals who do study demonology are in fact demonologists, but rather they want to have the knowledge at hand for themselves or for their paranormal group.

Demonology has been a "boom" subject in the paranormal community since some of the television ghost-hunting shows made it the focal point of

varied episodes. Many individuals do not necessarily think their home has a spirit in it, but *now* think there is a demon present. Even after all the evaluations and investigations, some clients will still insist *it* is some form of a demon that is tormenting their family – even without the solid evidence. This makes it even harder for the investigator and/or the demonologist.

Remember, not everything is caused by spirits and not everything is caused by a demonic entity. In some of these cases, when a client does keep insisting their problem involves a demonic entity, sadly, reasons may be due to their desire to be seen on television. Just be aware of this; some clients become upset when they do not see the film crew arriving to their home or area. It happens.

Too, it can happen the other way around. A so-called demonologist arrives at a client's home with a film crew trying to get a television spot or their own show. If it is an educational documentary, that might be a better reason; but just to get one's name and face on television is disgusting to most serious investigators and it is our opinions (and others) that this kind of individual needs to reevaluate themselves and their goals a bit better.

There is no fame or money in becoming a demonologist; this is a field to help people and not try to make money off the client or the client's situation. True, demonic cases take time to prove, gathering all physical evidence, having the client sign the proper medical release forms, talking to their family doctors or psychologists, interviewing family members and even their neighbors in some cases. There is a lot that goes into proving whether a demonic case is, in fact, a "real" case, and there is no room for those who are just thrill seekers.

Many of us who work in the paranormal realm have seen a huge jump in the numbers of individuals who are now "labeling" themselves as a demonologist. This is a tricky subject because there is no such thing as a "certified" demonologist. Many do not have the proper training in this field or the field experience, and many individuals find that the word "demonologist" is just cool to use.

There have been cases when a so-called demonologist went into a client's home and told the client without any type of evaluation, interview, or investigation, that there were demons in the home and then left, leaving the client in total terror and not knowing who to turn to next for help. This is NOT A GAME! Clients come to us for help, guidance, or advice, and to do such a thing is appalling. What happens if, for instance, the client *did* have some form of demonic activity in the home? The so-called demonologist has no experience or training and has no clue what to do next. Now the individual just put themselves, crewmembers, and the client in serious danger. Is claiming to be something one is not worth a client's injury or perhaps even death? Think long and hard about that.

Each demonologist does work differently and many follow different religious belief systems. Each case is different, as well, just as a paranormal investigator's cases are different each time. For many demonologists, there are cases of mental illness, drug and alcohol abuse, psychological issues, medication issues, sexual or psychical abuse, and so on. These cases always seem to start out with individuals claiming they have demons in their home, demons in certain objects, demonic possession within their own bodies or their children's, and animals are possessed by a demon of some sort

Do *you* know what to do in these matters? Hope so, if you are calling yourself a demonologist. I personally know many wonderful paranormal investigators who know more on the subject at hand than some individuals claiming to be demonologists. How does that look to a client? How does that look to the paranormal community? Not very good! It's best for the paranormal community to monitor those calling themselves demonologists when they are not, so that those who have the real skills are not discriminated against.

For myself, I have been challenged more times than I can count about my qualifications in the field of demonology and I welcome that. Everyone needs to do the research on an individual who is labeling themselves as a demonologist (or anything else, for that matter). I have been on other "demonologists' black lists" for working in the area of occult sciences. Without understanding just what type of work I do in the occult, many will try and talk or make hurtful comments. Usually these faux demonologists will need to seek out a person who really understands and is suitably trained in the field – someone who is truly a demonologist. I'm thankful that I've been able to help clients when others have failed in these undertakings.

Do the historical research, because one will find that many of the first "demonologists" were also occultists and exorcists. In the beginning of my demonology career, I was even looked over by many because of being a *female* demonologist. But that *did* quickly change when it was noted that I knew exactly what I was talking about, solved the toughest cases, and had twenty years of the field service. Know this: There is no such word as "fun" to a demonologist. It's long nights and piles of cases that come in every day and night. This work should be taken very seriously, for another individual's life could be in *your* hands if you choose to become involved with this particular line. You must ask yourself: Am I honestly ready for such a responsibility?

There is much preparation required. My personal background is much different; my qualifications are also much different than most. But it is just a small fraction of my background and qualifications on the subject of being a demonologist. I have a medical and law enforcement background, studied and trained with the top occult teachers in the world from the age of 19 to the present (and continue to study). I've examined the different religions of the world and how each of their belief systems worked, including their tools and prayers, and worked and studied under many of these religious leaders. I am called into many occult crime cases by local authorities, media, and families of victims to help solve, evaluate, and profile a situation. I receive many cases dealing with haunted objects or a beginner in the magical arts who tried to take on a ritual that they were not trained to do. I deal with symbols from all religions from magical orders to gang symbols. With this knowledge and training, I in turn help those with mild to extreme cases.

Please obtain the proper education, and train under another reputable demonologist.

- Do not just "label" yourself with the title of demonologist without really being one
- Do not think that just by reading books on the subject of demonology will, or can, make a you a demonologist or give you the tools to go out on a case, or deem a case "demonic," nor try to cast an entity out of an object or even another individual.
- Ask questions, because in some cases, knowledge really is power.

Following is a list of the most common signs of a demonic haunting. If a client or paranormal group experiences any of these items or feels that their case is one that the group cannot handle on their own, please contact a professional who is experienced in this area.

Common Signs of a Demonic Haunting

1. Foul smells
2. Religious objects disappear or become desecrated
3. Large objects teleporting to another room or area
4. Odd lights
5. Spontaneous fires break out and disappear within minutes without any trace or evidence
6. Restless sleep or being woken up every hour or more
7. Scratches or strange writing on the body that disappear within two to four hours
8. High pitch screams
9. Strange black cloud-like figures
10. Sudden violent behavior
11. Sudden thoughts of suicide
12. Sudden bursts of depression or feelings of isolation
13. Animals suddenly become violently sick or die
14. Walls inside a house or area seem to breathe
15. Loss of communication or sudden interruptions with phone lines
16. Violent nightmares

Paranormal Television Shows
and Movie Influences

"Vanity is my favorite sin...."

~Al Pacino, Actor
The Devil's Advocate, 1997

The first horror movie, which was only about two minutes long, was made by imaginative French filmmaker Georges Melies, titled *Le Manoir Du Diable* (1896) (aka *The Devil's Castle/The Haunted Castle*) containing familiar elements of later horror and vampire films: a flying bat, a medieval castle, a cauldron, a demon figure and skeletons, ghosts, witches, and a crucifix to dispatch the evil. Things have come a long way since 1896, with both technology and imagination. In 2008, the average cost to make a movie was $106 million dollars. The mind-blowing, high budget horror movie with tons of special effects drives that cost up even more. The average cost to make a reality-television series is $100,000. The prices may seem steep but the production companies are raking in the money, and lots of it with paying sponsors, merchandising rights, and product placement. But how exactly does the motion picture and television industry keep us all hooked on our "favorites?" Answer: Writers. There is a certain chemistry of directors, producers, story writers, and assistants that keep the entertainment ball rolling, and yes, we are referring to reality-television shows as well.

The first reality television show debuting in 1948, was Allen Funt's hidden camera *Candid Camera* show, broadcasting unsuspecting, ordinary people reacting to pranks. Other forerunners of modern reality television were the 1970s productions *The Dating Game*, *The Newlywed Game*, and *The Gong Show*, all of which featured participants who were eager to sacrifice some of their privacy and dignity in a televised competition. More modern shows include *Survivor* and *Real World*, both forcing people to live and compete with each other under certain circumstances. On every channel, we can now see average people competing down the runway, singing their hearts out, and yes, even ghost hunting. Individuals across the planet continue to delve into the reality drama and participate in near worship of the individuals appearing on the television screen.

The explosion of reality-based shows has paved the way for easy celebrity opportunity for individuals willing to sacrifice their reputation, integrity, and life as they used to know it. Unfortunately, in most cases, behind the scenes editing of these popular shows does not exactly scream to viewers that everything is not what it is cracked up to be. They force people into contrived situations. They deliberately select people who will react to certain situations in dramatic or uncontrolled environments. The footage is then edited, suspenseful music is added and one now has the cocktail of a reality-television show served up to them. This story writing does not necessarily imply that the show is faked. There very well may be a individual on an island with little food and water who competed in a competition for prizes, and won. What we do not see is the fact that the competitions were practiced by all contestants and in between filming takes.

So why are there story writers if it is reality television? If it was not for the story writers, there would be a whole lot of boring scenes televised. Competitions, drama, cast, cast changes, even bringing back a former guest to mix things up are all normal parts of television life nowadays. It is now accepted for some sort of the drama and excitement to be programmed into a plot. The downside of this kind of creative directing is that the cast dynamic can either blossom or fall apart. With producers wanting the audience to either love or hate a cast member, it can be done easily by enhancing the footage to sway people in any direction they want.

On TV

Both Katie and I have been on television and know how the production process works. In my own personal case, honestly I wish more scenes that I filmed with *Ghost Hunters International* displayed the real Shannon Sylvia. The scenes that were filmed of Brian Harnois and me provoking on the top of a snowy castle top, or the scenes where I was teaching a cast member how to read a temperature gauge properly were all deleted. The Shannon Sylvia that everyone has come to know *now* is a thick-skinned, intelligent woman – not the scared girl with the goose bumps standing in the corner. So was I a victim of typecasting? One could answer *yes* to that question. By choosing to go on television to showcase talents in ghost hunting, I was faced with some of the most difficult challenges a person could face. There was constant scrutiny by strangers on the websites using "keyboard courage" to throw about insults, and criticism peaked after the shows aired. The challenge of having to balance my company back at home with my travel time, up to four weeks in Europe away from the world, can be a big obstacle for anyone. I had to ultimately make a choice: pursue television or stay in Massachusetts and go back to my workaholic lifestyle. I chose the latter. My career in design is something I will have the rest of my life, something I can fall back on. Ghost hunting on television is a flash in the pan and everyone's time is eventually up. I can be myself with my friends and family at home and not have to worry about what the rest of the world will think of me or criticize my every move.

On the flip side, many positive things can come from being on a television show. It is what the individual makes of it, and because of that, I have been fortunate in many ways. Being on a hit cable television show has opened many doors for me that normally would have been closed. I have amazing opportunities to investigate locations across the country with guest investigators and am enjoying meeting every new face and answering every question, whether or not I have heard it a million times before. I was asked in 2008 to be a professional college speaker and my agent sends me to the most remarkable University and State schools to speak in front of students about my work. I am blessed to have made so many friends in the field, even other television personalities who are on hand at a moment's notice to attend a charity event to raise money for unfortunate families. Being a part of so much has really helped me realize that I do have talents, and I do have a ton of supporters, fans, and friends throughout the field and outside the field. I started out in this field at an early age trying to learn everything I could about the paranormal and now I teach others about the subject. Honestly and from the heart, people tell me how they truly appreciate it. For that, I feel my time on a television show was not wasted.

Camera Rolling!

The word "paranormal" has exploded; every television channel has some form of show on the subject now – individuals investigating haunted homes and creepy locations. Many paranormal groups today are born because of these types of shows, and many groups may be misleading because of those same shows. We all from time to time have dealt with a few paranormal groups who saw a television show and suddenly go into a client's home and provoke a spirit, doing more harm than good for the client. Watch the paranormal shows, but please remember that there is production involved with the making of many shows. Watch a show for the entertainment factor and do not believe everything you see or hear.

There is a lot of downtime during the investigations and if the producer sees a reaction on a cast member's face or a guest on the show, they will ask for the person to reenact the action or comment for the film crew. We have seen shows that blow a subject way off course, and again the calls and emails come flooding in, asking is this subject, in fact, real.

When one is contacted to be a guest or a cast member on the show, a contract is signed. The producer and production company have full rights to air the parts in any way they may choose, which could be editing the film or blending a part of the filming which seems to fit better into a scene.

The Fame Game

Fame and fortune are not to be found working on a ghost hunter television show. It is so easy to land a spot on television nowadays, but there are good points and bad points to this opportunity. On one hand, the individual needs to know that the pay is either nothing but the expenses to come out to film or a very small stipend to be a regular on a recurring show.

Risking one's home and work life is a hefty price to pay to either see your reputation rise like a shining star or plummet like a falling star. We have seen people lose jobs thinking that they would have a career in paranormal investigating, then come back from filming to being unemployed.

Jealousy and greed are two monsters no one wants to fight and it is all too common on the set of a television show. How many times have we seen a person or team who has made a cameo spot on a television show featuring them as the celebrity guest at a paranormal event or conference? Their fifteen seconds of fame have come and gone, but now the individual or individuals are selling posters with their autographs on them. It does make one wonder exactly what their motive was in the first place. Now Katie has a story that will take us into another side on just how the television world really works.

How it Really Goes

There was a show where I was contacted by producers to come in to be interviewed and share some education on a certain entity, which I gladly agreed to do. Education is important and I personally saw no harm in appearing on the show. Let me make myself very clear at this point, no one spoke to me about the case or the paranormal group or clients who were involved in this particular show. I fulfilled my part and traveled a few hours back home from the filming location.

Suddenly, I began receiving emails because of the show's episode and I was being asked: "Why did you not help the clients?" I was rather devastated to find out the producer had clipped certain parts of the episode and make it seem like the paranormal group had called me in personally to help on the case. I, in fact, had never even met the group or shared any contact with them.

So one can see now and understand the misleading process of the world of television. It is a "Catch 22." Help the viewer understand a subject on the paranormal better, and, at the same time, mislead the viewer.

On many occasions, television producers have contacted me to make guest appearances and even have my own television shows covering my work as a demonologist to share certain cases with the viewer. Kindly, I tend to decline, due to not believing in exploiting my clients or to have each victim relive the encounter. (Hasn't the client been through enough trauma already?) The thought of displaying these cases for an entertainment purpose just is not right, in my own opinion. Having the client sit in a dark room with cameras pointed at them can be a very stressful situation – not to mention the privacy of the case would be gone. Perhaps some people will call me foolish for declining such opportunities, thereby gaining more respect by my peers, but either way, I personally sleep very well at night with my decisions.

Cheating to be on TV

Let's touch on another rather sensitive subject: Investigators lying about cases and stealing other's evidence to get themselves, or their paranormal group, on a certain television show – or to have their own show. Do not act so surprised when we bring such a topic up. Those of us in the paranormal field see these issues happen all the time. As mentioned earlier on relating to trademarks, I had a fellow go to the extremes of trying to *sell* my trademarked paranormal group's name to networks because he wanted his own show, which was airing at the time on a local cable-access station. My lead investigator heard of this and brought it to our attention. We, in turn, immediately contacted the proper channels and showed proof of owning the trademark for the name. The individual had his show yanked from the station right away.

What blew me away was our group had been running a show, airing for many years on the cable-access channel, and had decided to take a break from filming due to my overloaded schedule. Local cable-access stations do not look up show names (paranormal or otherwise) at the trademark website. This is the reasonability of the person who is taking accountability for the show. The person having the show signs an agreement that no trademark or copyright infringements are being violated and the penalty falls on the owner of the show and not the station.

No Cool Kids' Club

In conclusion, television will not make an individual or their paranormal team part of the cool kids' club. It can backfire and cause more rifts and problems than one could possibly handle. Making a good name for one's team is what it is all about, and if television happens and it's the right time, then fate will treat the team well. One can still have a voice, with all the Internet radio shows available and social media networking sites out there today. Do not forget the reasons why we all became interested in the paranormal in the first place; too many already have.

PART II

Extraterrestrial Life

"If I become President, I'll make every piece of information this country has about UFO sightings available to the public and scientists. I am convinced that UFOs exist because I have seen one."

**~President Jimmy Carter
During his presidential campaign, 1976.**

Aliens Among Us

Even the Vatican, in 2008, stated that there is some form of intelligent life outside of our earth's atmosphere. But what, in fact, *are* aliens and where do these "beings" come from? Most definitions of the word *alien* are basically the same: a form of a life that is assumed to live or exist outside of earth's solar system. Who are we, as humans, to really state that there are no other life forms that visited earth or other planets in the past, within the solar systems? We cannot be the only type of life form around, and honestly, the evidence of other intelligent life has been around for many centuries.

Author Eric Von Däniken has written many books about the ancient alien theories. Eric presents theories with actual information about the influence aliens have had on our human culture, along with picture evidence. There have been movies, television shows, and books all with alien themes. The subject is not an old one, and even though many of us, perhaps, are scared to know the truth, it is a fascinating subject. It does make one think we are, and were, definitely not the only species on earth. Of course, there will always be skeptics and non believers of such subject matters, but is the idea really that farfetched?

A Theory on the Origins of UFOs
By David J. Manch

Having lived in the Western Massachusetts area all my life, I am thankful for the pristine skylines under which I can ply my search for proof of the existence of UFOs and their alien occupants. But are UFOs (and their pilots) truly visitors from another world, or is there another explanation which accounts for their appearances over the millennia? Taking into consideration that the star nearest to our own is Alpha Centauri, at 4.3 light years away, you can form the argument that even a technologically superior race may not be able to span that distance in a tiny spaceship, despite theories on bending space-time, wormhole travel, and antimatter drives. It is more probable that UFOs have traveled a far less distance...coming from an entirely different universe altogether, which just happens to be parallel to our own.

Stanford University cosmologist Andrei Linde has theorized that new universes can be created by branching off from our own and existing in very close proximity to us. This is the *Multiverse Theory*, and it states that parallel universes may have developed at a much greater pace to our own, and therefore the far more advanced "humans" in one of our neighboring universes may have found a way to exploit the thin barrier that separates

us, allowing them to travel into our universe. Are the aliens we believe to be visiting us from another world actually from a universe which parallels our own? Are the "aliens" actually far more advanced humans that have bridged the gap in the universes to study our way of life? We may never know for sure, but the possibilities are equally endless and fascinating.

David Manch majored in biochemistry at the University of New Hampshire and wrote his first research paper on the paranormal while a student there in 1982. A veteran law enforcement officer, David was the Senior Advisor to New England Paranormal, and has taught classes on the paranormal at many locations throughout New England. He also has appeared on a number of paranormal television shows, including *Ghosts R-NEAR* with Keith and Sandra Johnson. For the past six years, David has conducted an annual outing at various haunted locations, open to the general public and free of charge. His book, *There Are Ghosts In Our World* can be found at his website: www.earthboundphantom.com.

Types of Aliens

Greys

There seem to be many different types of aliens that have been documented by individuals who claim to have been abducted by them. The most common recorded sightings or abductions come from the type called Greys. These gray-in-color aliens are supposedly the same species that crashed in Roswell, New Mexico in 1947. There are many who claim that these aliens visit earth to guide humans and keep track of our advancement in technology and evolution growth.

Others believe these Greys are abducting humans for unknown experiments and breeding purposes. There are those individuals who do think that they have an agreement with our government: humans for alien technology.

Those encountering these Greys seem to report the same description of them: body is rather thin with an over-large head, small, slit mouth, and no ears. Some individuals report being spoken to by some form of mental telepathy. Large, black oval-shaped eyes with no eye lids have also been mentioned. Their skin is gray in color with skin texture almost like a dolphin's skin with no hair (in cases, the skin is wrinkled in texture), and height ranges from four feet to six feet. It seems as there are only four fingers on each hand and these are sometimes web shaped in nature. Some individuals (such as ufologists, abductees, and government officials) state that this alien race does not have organs in the same way humans do, nor do they have a respiratory and digestive system. Also, there is no evidence of sexual organs. Some believe Greys have two brains which give them the higher intelligence that allows the ability to "suspend" an individual in the air, totally motionless, during abduction. There are many theories, but one intriguing theory is that the Greys use (much like the dolphin species) a type of sonic wave blast to "stun" their victims or prey.

Supposedly, these gray-type aliens were created by another alien race called the Reptilians for the sole purpose of being a slave race. Some individuals state there was a type of uprising between the Greys and their creators, causing the Greys to flee, traveling through the galaxy until they landed on earth. Still others believe them to be humans from the future, a product of Nazi experiments – there are claims that these kinds of experiments are still going on today.

Roswell Daily Record, July 8, 1947.

There are so many theories and claims as to where and who the gray aliens really are. Were the Greys dying and did they find that only the minerals on earth could help them survive? Are they trying to breed with humans to create a new hybrid race? Lots of questions, but do we truly know the answers? Will we ever? Could the answers be right in front of us, but we as a society are afraid to know the truth?

There have been many television programs and movies dedicated to this subject, along with books, such as author Whitley Strieber, who claims to have been abducted by this type of alien in his popular book *Communion*. He calls these aliens "Zetas" from the Zeta Reticuli star system.

Reptilian

Does sound like a monster from a science fiction movie, huh? Indeed, but there have been many accounts of encounters with the reptoids, as many individuals call these creatures (others call them "lizard people"). Throughout time, our ancestors have drawn pictures and even made clay images of such creatures that came down from the heavens; some helped the human race, others tried to harm us.

These reptoids seem to be a similar height to humans, and in some cases, can be up to nine feet tall, with "snake-like," scaly skin covering their bodies and faces like that of a reptile we see in pet stores and in the wild today. Some abductees have reported these creatures also look like the "praying mantis" in their appearance. This is actually wrong as the Praying Mantis-like creatures are believed to be a completely different species of alien altogether. There has been a lot of confusion regarding this particular being as reports are rare and there are some discrepancies among those who have made them. Reports are slim, but do exist.

Is there more than one race of these reptoids out there in our universe or hiding deep within our underground caverns? Some claim reptoids are, in fact, from our Planet Earth and are not such an enemy to our race; others are supposedly hiding deep within our earth. Without solid evidence, everything is just a theory, until otherwise proven.

Now, on the flip side of this subject, there are some individuals who claim there is another type of reptoid that comes from a planet close to a bright star in the Draco constellation which is very aggressive in nature towards humans. These look almost the same, but have wings and horns that come from the spine and sometimes penetrate through the skull of the creature. The Draco, as some individuals have labeled this reptilian creature, is an enemy that our human race needs to look out for because the agenda is not to make peace with Planet Earth or humans.

The reptilians seem to abduct humans in a different way than the gray aliens; with the Greys, a human is physically abducted, but with the Reptilians, it is more of the mind. In fact, they abduct the human mind through manipulation which can be through nightmares and violent sexual dreams that have emotions. Feeding off human negative emotions is what gives this alien race fuel and power. We cannot state yes or no such action does or doesn't take place; most of us do believe in some form of "paranormal" does exist out there in the world and planets beyond ours – so why not this? Our history through mythological, biblical, and cultural times has shown some form of text which was written about "beings or gods" that were far greater than our own human race. Could every culture and every era through time be wrong about such encounters and abductions? Highly unlikely; but as a society, we look at solid facts. So again I ask: Are the answers in front of us; do we just choose not to look?

Nordic

Nords, or Nordic aliens as most call this type, are reported to be beautiful in nature, taller than the average human being, and seem to have the characteristics of pale skin, blond hair, and blue or green eyes. Some contactees have reported the Nords wearing a tight body-type suit and others report seeing them in a white-type robe. Some of the earliest reports of these beings were from the 1950s and 1960s; after that it seems that reports became more scattered and less publicized. However, I do believe there have been continued interactions, and as of recently, more people are coming out as saying that they have been contacted or that they even channel these beings, The Nords. Contactee reports state the aliens were from the planet Venus and came to observe the human race without interfering; and most encounters are with the male aliens who seem to communicate through telepathy with a soft smooth voice, meant to relax us. More recent reports show that the Nords are greatly concerned with our welfare and whether we have become a more open society. Their interest also includes issues regarding our planet being in crisis and most experiencers have claimed that the Nordics have tried to forewarn of future disasters and give important messages regarding global issues.

Visitations and Abductions

"...despite the fact that we humans are great collectors of souvenirs, not one of these persons claiming to have been aboard a flying saucer has brought back so much as an extraterrestrial tool or artifact, which could, once and for all, resolve the UFO mystery."

~Philip Klass

Aliens are not prejudice about who is abducted; there are reports around the world of every type of human and every varied age becoming the victim of abduction. Many individuals who have been abducted have found small micro-type chips inside their bodies, which some feel is a tracking device and collecting information. We will get more into that subject in a minute. But we must (as any researcher) analyze the facts, such as whether the victim is suffering from a true alien abduction or something else. What about sleep paralysis? Some of the symptoms are very similar, such as not being able to move or scream out for help or feelings of a presence in the same area. Hypnosis is another root which some abductees take to try and remember the incident which occurred. But going deep into the subconscious mind could be a dangerous action to take; some individuals feel this too subjective for the victim. Are the memories truly that of the victim or a planted memory from an article or television show the individual had seen years ago or even that day? We are not stating one answer is the right answer or that there is no such thing as alien abductions, but again, we must look at the whole picture.

What are these strange objects that many abductees seem to have implanted inside their bodies? Many abductees report that while being abducted, they are sometimes stripped of their clothes and are placed upon what seems to be a type of operating table. They're on a cold metal table; horrific experiments are conducted on the victim, and there may be removal of body fluids and samples of body tissues. Blood, saliva, sperm, and even samples of a woman's ovaries which include the taking out of samples of the eggs, have been reported. Some recall being in pain as the procedures are being done. An oral liquid is given to the victim before the probing starts; others have reported a liquid-type substance placed on the areas that are being examined. There has not been evidence, as we know, of that the liquid-type agent being found on any of the abductees' bodies tested; thoughts are that the aliens did remove all evidence before returning the abductees.

Before each abductee is returned, small unknown materials, which seem to work like a micro-tracking device, are placed inside the body. Such places have been in the feet, behind the eye lids, up the naval cavity, back of the neck, genitals and even in the arms. The true function of this tiny device (of which only a few have been supposedly collected by humans) is still being studied by scientists and researchers, but one theory is that it is for tracking humans. Other theories are that it is for harvesting humans for food and for reproductive purposes in mixing our DNA with theirs to create a new hybrid race or to save their own race. The less "threatening" theory is that it is their beaming reception device; people who have implants like this will be able to be brought on the ship in the event of a polar shift or other catastrophe that threatens the planet as a whole.

We all have our own thoughts as to the real reasons we, as humans, are being abducted, but will we ever know the truth? We can only hope someday we will know that answer.

Most Common Signs of Alien Contact/Abductions

Note: Please seek medical attention from your physician before jumping to any conclusions that this is, in fact, a connection to being abducted by aliens.

Below is a list with descriptions of the signs which most abductees might encounter or experience before or after contact; these are the most commonly reported. Abduction can take place at any moment and anytime of the day or night.

Strange marks on body

Odd irritation markings, such as in a triangular pattern, scoop-like markings on the body, laser-like markings, typically in geometric patterns, and unexplained objects imbedded in the back of the neck and head, particularly in the nasal cavity have been reported.

Unexplained medical symptoms

Issues with sinus, sudden headaches, sudden nose bleeds, back issues, and sudden neck problems have been reported as a sign.

Insomnia

Sudden loss of normal sleeping patterns or fear of falling asleep can be an indication.

Ringing in ears

Many abductees claim to hear a ringing in the ears right before and after being abducted.

Increased dreaming

Dreams focusing around flying or floating in the air, through windows and doors can be an indicator.

Flashbacks

Some individuals experience flashbacks of their abduction, which show glimpses, but not usually full detail. While under hypnosis, most abductees can then describe in full detail their accounts of abductions, but sometimes the more horrific or secret details are screened.

Cosmic awareness

Sudden knowledge of the stars and planets in the universe that the individual had no prior knowledge of can be a sign.

Sexual/relationship issues

Sudden withdrawal from family and friends, and even sexual encounters with spouses become more difficult.

Implants

Small microchips found in the sinus cavity, neck, or even inside the brain that can't be explained can be an indicator. There is no knowledge regarding how or why the object could be inside the individual. Some claim this microchip is a tracking device that keeps tabs on the abductees.

Strange balls of light following or in and around the home

Some encounter flashes of lights which follow them from place to place or are seen within the home. People have reported seeing such lights right before the abduction occurs.

Witness to the encounter or abduction

Many people have claimed to be a witness to someone else being abducted, but not themselves.

Lost time or black outs

Actions or experiences are not recalled right before and during abduction.

Crop Circles and Formations

Crop circles are rather intriguing to many individuals due to the fact that the makers of such designs are unknown. These crop designs are usually made overnight by flattening crops (wheat, rye, oat, corn stocks and many other such substances) in a variety of shapes and styles. Another strange occurrence with these crop circles and formations is the evidence of no disturbance in the making, such as breaking the stems of the crops that form the patterns. There seems to be some type of force making the textures bend as the swirling forms are placed. Each design is different and range in size from small to extremely large in diameter. Strange circle designs, animal designs, insects, and even human shapes can be found all around the world. Some individuals suggest this is or might be done by some form of heat, or a burst of heat, which makes the texture easier to swirl into a pattern. But if this is the case, again we do not know, or cannot find, the heating source that causes such high temperatures to leave the crop circles so quickly.

Are the formations a map of some kind for the aliens' knowledge? Could it be a map to show where to land or what type of minerals or resources are in that area? Is it a labeling system or their version of a billboard like we see with advertising as we drive down the street?

There have been some crop circles that have been proven to be a hoax, but most of the designs have been unexplained and are not made by the human hand or any human kind of technology. The peak of the interest of crop formations did not hit the public's curiosity until the 2002 movie came out called *Signs*. This is not an new subject; in fact, eye witnesses go as far back as the 1500s and perhaps even further.

Many do believe that these formations are made by ultrasound, which is on a high-level frequency channel. This type of frequency level can also be found in sacred sites that are made out of stone and even at the pyramids. The eyewitnesses claim to see a bright light over the crop area and hear strange noises coming from the light. Suddenly, this light is gone and there in the crop field are some of the most incredible crop

Crop circle in a cornfield in Wiltshire, England.

formation designs. If these formations are, in fact, made by other-worldly beings, then is the theory of ultrasound and sound waves that obscure? Extraterrestrials are far more advanced than humans and sound waves have long been a theory as to how the Egyptian Pyramids were made. So why not the crop formations as well? Those who visit these sites report feeling dizzy, anxious, peaceful, strange tingles in their bodies, and an odd buzzing type of noise.

There are individuals who spend their time debunking the crop circles, re-making the formations with a team and a "stomping board" which helps in the pressing down of the crops. On an average, it can take up to five or more hours to construct a crop circle design. The individuals who are making such crop circles are really cashing in on the idea; big corporations are now paying to have such individuals make company logos in the crop fields for advertising. What is missing from these hoaxes are the strange lights and the odd noises that eyewitnesses have reported where, within minutes, a formation is made and the lights and sounds are gone.

Many have come forward and admitted to making these formations, but again, no mention of falsifying the strange lights and sounds. Is it just a hoax to gain the attention of the media and visitors? Is this just a chance for some individuals to cash in on the hype of the crop circle phenomena? As we stated before, yes, there are some crop circle hoaxes, but who made the formations that even the scientists are puzzled about?

Making a Crop Circle of Your Own

1. Find a good location. (Remember to follow private property laws.)
2. Create a design on paper that will be the crop circle.
3. Once at the location, measure out the circle.
4. Have one individual stand in the middle of the soon-to-be circle and use one foot to push down the crops that will be used to make the formation and the other foot to remain stationary at the center.
5. Use a long piece of rope about 4 feet long or larger that is tied at both ends to a board which is the stalk stomper. One individual will stay inside the circle and the other individual or individuals will then walk all around the edge of the circle, placing one foot in the middle of the stalk stomper board and stomping down.

Unidentified Flying Objects

"I can assure you that flying saucers, given that they exist, are not constructed by any power on earth."

~**President Harry S. Truman**
1950

Aliens are synonymous with flying saucers and lights in the sky; this phenomena has been occurring since 47000 BC in Hunan, China. The first well-documented sighting took place in Nuremberg, Germany in the year 1561. A broadsheet from that time described a battle taking place in the sky between balls, plates, tube shapes, and crosses of red, blue, and black objects. Observed by the entire town, this was the first well-written and organized piece of evidence and experience; it is still studied and looked at today by dedicated ufologists.

The actual term "flying saucer" was first invented by businessman Kenneth Arnold to describe what he was seeing when he was flying his private plane near Washington's Mt. Rainier in 1947. He claimed to have seen nine different objects flying in formation over and around the mountain at speeds of over 1,600 miles per hour. In a report, he described the objects to be "like a saucer skipping over water." Later, this was shortened to the now-popular term flying saucer.

In the 1960s, the UFO craze really took off and panels of scientists convened to try to get to the bottom of the phenomena. These experts found, after reviewing the gathered evidence, that most (if not all) of the sightings were easily explained by natural occurrences or outright hoaxes. Not all of the scientific community agreed with the panel's conclusions – some challenging that the group refused to look at the cases that were not so easily explained away, or if they *did* look at those cases, they were not definitive in their answers. So this led the mainstream scientific community to believe that yes there may be life out there, that since the most reliable of the cases, such as that of Clarence Johnson, an aerospace engineer, could not be explained so easily, then there must be some truth to it.

Multiple-witness events are the hardest to dismiss, but they don't always occur en masse like that. Shannon has shared two stories of what are believed to be UFO encounters.

A Strange Sun

In the summertime of 1984, my friend and I had a great day of shopping at the mall, a barbeque, and later on, a sleepover. School vacation was almost over and trying to sleep in the hot August heat was unbearable, so we wanted to venture outside the house as gingerly as we could without getting caught. Rosalie and I took some Cabbage Patch Kids dolls that best looked like our own hair color, stuffed them under blankets with pillows, and allowed their corn silk hair to dangle out a little to trick my mother who may peek in the living room into our sleeping quarters. It was 11:30 p.m., and all we wanted to do was get some fresh air and be able to talk about boys, life, and the pursuit of happiness without being scolded for still being up so late at night.

We found a comfortable spot on the freshly tarred road outside my house about fifty feet away from the door where we'd escaped and parked ourselves there to chat a while. We faced each other in the street so I could see all the way to the end of my neighborhood and she could see the opposite direction. I looked up behind Rosalie and high in the trees over the red house, five houses down from mine, was an enormous "sun" glowing in the sky. It was a dark orange color unlike anything I'd ever seen before. Just as fast as I told her to turn around to look at it, it swooped very quickly behind the trees and roofline and disappeared. It was the approximate size of the sun, if you saw it over the house, but much closer in proximity. For this glowing circular object to swoop so quickly and disappear, I knew it was neither the sun nor the moon. To this day, I don't know what it was, but it sure as hell bothered me.

Funny Lights

The second experience I had was in 1997. I'd just graduated from college and I was living in a brand new three-story duplex in Fitchburg, Massachusetts at the site of a former fraternity house that had burned down. It was high on a hill with a glamorous view of the city surrounded by big, beautiful Victorian homes. I was living there alone, waitressing many hours to make the rent and car payments on time. My Dalmatian, Milow, was always by my side in this big place, barking at every person who walked by or every noise in the neighborhood.

I stayed home that night not wanting to go out, I was watching *The Wizard of Oz* on television and sipping a massive glass of chocolate milk with a straw. Bundled on the couch, wrapped in a blanket, Milow was snuggled next to me. Suddenly, she jumped off the couch and began barking at the picture window, which was in the second-story living room. I didn't think anything of it because there was always a lot of foot traffic on my street due to the apartments at the end of the road. She continued to bark, so I went to the window to check to see if I had an unannounced visitor.

At the window I saw at eye level, a white light the size of a tennis ball, and it was pulsing. I first thought it was a toy a child was using down below or some sort of flashlight, but my thoughts turned to panic when the light began zooming very fast away from my window, then back to where I was standing, dog barking and all. It flew up into the trees across the street perhaps eighty feet tall at a very fast rate, back and forth, left and right, up and down. It then flew up into the sky and disappeared.

I ran to the phone and called my father who laughed and asked me what I was drinking; he told me there was really nothing we could do about the funny lights. I thought of calling the police, but being a waitress in town, I did not want to get off on the wrong foot with crazy UFO stories coming from me. I had nowhere to go; I shut the television off, ran upstairs to my bedroom, grabbed Milow and some rosary beads, pulled the blankets over my head, and prayed until I fell asleep.

The next day was life as usual; I told a few people my experience but no one ever came forward with a story that sounded similar to what I saw. I have spoken to some UFO researchers who are familiar with this "orb UFO," where it basically gathers information, though this is not proven. I have no idea what it was; I had no unusual marks on my body or memories of abduction after the sighting. I can tell you, though, like the large orb in the sky that looked like the sun at nighttime, I know what I saw and I know it was not something normal. It was out of the ordinary, and in my opinion, it was an Unidentified Flying Object.

Katie's story, on the other hand, had multiple witnesses. She was just one of many in our county who observed a UFO. The local radio station received many calls about it and so it has become a reliable case in the eyes of local ufologists. Here is what Katie experienced:

My story is not all little green men, but guess why not share it anyway! I was a young teenage, around 15 years old, living in Goffstown. My dear friend, Chris, and I were walking home to my house from a local pizza place, which was down the road. It was not late at night and the sun was about to go down; there was still some daylight left.

As we walked passed a street right before my own street, suddenly, right out of nowhere, hovered an oval-shaped flying object. I swore if we jumped that we could have touched the craft. I saw three lights on the front of the odd-shaped object, but did not notice any type of window or cockpit where a pilot would normally sit. Chris and I just stood there, and right before our eyes, the flying object took off so fast that we could not tell where it went.

We, of course being young, decided to call up the local radio station and share our strange encounter. It seems there were many reports around our area giving the same description of the unidentified flying object. For a short time after the incident, I did have a dream of a bright light and of being in a café. I remember in this dream that I was hiding behind the counter and some people started screaming, and then I woke up. Were my friend and I abducted? I honestly do not think we were, but some people may disagree with me and feel we might have been. I have never had the dream nor encountered such an incident again.

Different Types of Ships

The ships described by people come in many different shapes, from the spherical to the triangular and cigar shapes. They also vary in size and in what they do. Here is a breakdown of the most popular UFO descriptions:

- Saucer – These ships are usually seen with a dull silver sheen to them.
- Hubcap
- Lenticular – Think of two bowls with the rims glued together.
- Flat top – Think of a straw hat and you've got the idea.
- Spheres
- Orange balls of light – Most commonly seen at nighttime.
- Spinning silver ball – Almost like a disco ball or silver Christmas tree ornament.
- Sphere with a ring – Band lays in the center of the sphere.
- Conical
- Top – Literally looks like a spinning top flying through the air.
- Hat – Ranging in sizes, it looks like a conical hat.
- Cylindrical – Often seen with the silver dull sheen or white with a glow to it.
- Faux Plane – Like an airplane without the wings.
- Oil Barrel – Much like a Faux Plane, but the ends stop abruptly rather than tapering.
- Triangular – Always black or charcoal gray, there are usually three lights on the underside.
- Equilateral – Shaped just like an equilateral triangle that flies (usually horizontally) through the air.
- Rounded – Similar shape to the equilateral but the edges are rounded.
- Diamond – Shaped just as it sounds.
- Manta Ray – Along the same lines as the triangle, it is often seen in black or dark colors.

There are so many variations of flying saucers that once you start identifying their shapes and sizes, it may be hard to keep up with them all. Aside from the ones mentioned in the lists above, there are also pyramid shapes, donuts, cross, hexagonal, and many more.

What do you do if you actually see a UFO? Report it, of course! This next part we will talk about how to observe and report a sighting!

Observation and Reporting

Pictures and video are always the icing on the cake when it comes to reporting UFO activity. Be sure to take video cameras and still cameras off the *auto focus* setting, so it won't blur when the camera tries to "lock" on the object. Also, make sure you can keep your camera steady, lean up against a tree or keep a tripod handy just for that purpose. Try to keep some reference points in view – whether you use a house, water tower, etc., this helps to show distance and size. If you can have reliable and reputable witnesses around you at the time of the filming, do so! If you are using a still camera, try to have negatives available for study as well as the camera itself – this way, possible defects can be ruled out. Sworn testimony is always a plus and should be required from the witnesses and camera operator.

If using digital equipment to document your evidence, such as a digital camera or camcorder, after downloading them, take the images straight from your computer; do not touch or alter them in any way, do not open them with a graphic design or photo-altering program. This way the researcher can verify that the source was the camera and not Photoshop. This same technique is encouraged for use by all investigators and witnesses in any type of paranormal phenomena – from cryptids to ghosts and UFOs.

In the ideal situation, with a most observant witness, they will provide answers to the following questions:

- The date, time, and how long the sighting occurred
- The location of the occurrence
- How many objects were there?
- What shapes were there?
- Were there any lights? If so what colors/patterns?
- How did they move and where did they move to?
- How big were they?
- How close or far away?
- At what angle were they? At what angle were you?
- What was the weather like?
- Other details, such as was a haze around the objects? Sounds? Did other objects come from the first one?

What is the point in observing UFOs if you have no one to investigate them? There are many UFO networks, the most popular being MUFON (Mutual UFO Network) which catalogs sightings and experiences around the world. NUFORC (National UFO Research Center) also does this. There are many regional groups and networks as well, so don't be afraid to explore your area. We have listed some of our favorites under the resources section of this book.

III

Supernatural Creatures

"We should never try to deny the beast — the animal within us."

~Dr. George Waggner
From 1981 movie: *The Howling*

Monsters Among Us

Creatures of the unexplained intrigue our minds, and the questions pour from our lips. Why can we only catch a glimpse of such creatures from time to time? Where do these creatures come from?

Movies and television show us just how far our imaginations can travel, but what about the cold hard facts. Cryptozoology is a fascinating subject of study of undiscovered animals and creatures that the science community has yet to determine "real," without solid, hard, factual proof. On the other hand, many crytozoologists turn away from the hunt of supernatural creatures or cryptids (another term used for unknown creatures first used by a man named John Wall in 1983), such as werewolves, or even creatures like the Mothman, in fear of being ridiculed by their colleagues.

It is more about science and biology when trying to find new animal species and collecting the data of eyewitness accounts. It has been paranormal investigators and like individuals who call themselves Bigfoot hunters who take more of an interest in the hunt for unexplained creatures. Even though the study of cryptozoology is not yet a legitimate branch of zoology, the two from time to time do work closely together.

Do these strange unknown creatures really exist? Why not? We have discovered many unknown creatures that have been roaming the earth since the planet went into existence. At one point in time people from the local villages were scared of a huge black and white monster that lived in the jungle. Today this creature is known to us as the Panda bear. Underwater sea creatures that were once thought to be extinct are now being discovered, from giant squids to fish and sharks. Maybe these creatures are intelligent and know all the right places to hide to keep from being discovered, or worse, hunted down and killed. There are too many sightings from every walk of life, from law enforcement officials to individuals just taking a hike into the woods or just driving home from work to not believe their encounters or attacks. Yes, there are individuals who believe that some of these strange creatures could have been trapped within rocks that were once tunnels or caves, and due to the earth plates shifting and causing earthquakes, those walls or entrances open and allow the creatures out. That is not a bad theory and could possibly happen – or perhaps already did. Until we can validate this theory and find proof, more expeditions and research will have to be done.

Bigfoot, Sasquatch, and The Yeti

There are no real differences between these three animals except for location and coloring.

Sasquatch was a term coined by Canadian J.W. Burns and is believed to be a mispronunciation of a native word for the mysterious biped. J.W. was a writer and teacher who worked on the Chehalis Reservation in British Columbia. There he heard stories about the Forest Fathers or Wild Ones. He made Sasquatch a household name through his writings, which included local papers, books, and even national magazines.

A part of a headline for an article in the *Humboldt Times* of Northwestern California is the first record of the word Bigfoot. Editor Andrew Genzoli was approached by resident Jerry Crew with a casting of the unusual print found in Bluff Creek Valley setting the name in stone. The word is used strictly in America and on the Canadian border.

Yeti is a term from Tibet used to describe the white-coated cousins of the mountain-climbing ape there. It has also been referred to as the Abominable Snowman due to its preference for colder climates and, at times, aggressive behaviors. They are believed to come in different sizes from small four- or five-foot sizes, all the way up to thirteen-foot monsters which are believed to have no compunction for eating humans.

Field Guide to Cataloging Evidence of Bigfoot

Yes, these hominids seems to show signs of intelligence. I think that has been displayed through the numerous encounters people have had over the years. Nevertheless, tracking this elusive biped is no different from tracking and hunting any other animal. There are certain things you need to be sure to take with you into the woods for your expedition.

For You

- Enough food to last the trip. You want to make sure it is well-preserved food if you are taking a weekend trip into the woods. Here are some suggestions: Ramen noodles, beef jerky, canned meat, juice boxes, dehydrated Fruit
- Tent
- Two-way radio

- Bug spray
- Map
- GPS
- Compass
- Flashlights
- Batteries
- Personal heater (depending on when and where you are going)
- Matches or lighter
- Canteen

For Evidence Collection

- Still camera
- Video camera
- Trail cam
- Casting ingredients
- Baiting supplies, such as apples, berries, acorns, fish, and grapes
- Pheromone Chips – These chips are a mix of ape and human pheromones and can be purchased at BlueNorth.com for $40 (at time of this publication). They are used by hanging them from tree branches.
- Thermographic camera

Plastering a Bigfoot Print

Casts of this elusive biped's feet are the most common form of evidence used to verify a bigfoot's existence. The Skookum cast is one of the most highly debated among the cryptid community, having collected hair samples that led to bear, elk, and one other mysterious animal fiber – it was pretty much a full-body cast of the animal. Skeptics say that evidence collected is of an animal natural to those particular woods – possibly a bear. Diehard researchers merely point to the evidence of a primate-like foot with the ankle.

But how does the novice Bigfoot/Sasquatch researcher gather footprints? It's simple enough! Here is what you need:

- Dental Stone (although if in a bind, Plaster of Paris will work, however, it degrades very quickly)
- Mixing Bowl
- Water
- Cardboard Strips
- Paper Clips or tape

Once you have found your bigfoot print, establish a perimeter of the cardboard strips around it. Try to make it oval in shape and give at least two inches of room around the track. Push the bottom edge of the cardboard firmly into the ground. This will brace your dental stone walls so it doesn't

Bigfoot Trap on Collings Mountain Trail near Applegates Lake in Jackson County Oregon. *Photo taken by Oregon nativist and arborist Mario D. Vaden www.mdvaden.com*

escape all over the ground. Be sure to overlap the edges of cardboard and put your paperclip or tape at that location so it forms a solid wall all the way around the print.

Next mix your dental stone in the mixing bowl; the ratio is 2:1 (two parts mix to one part water) – one cup mix to every half cup water, or for every two cups of mix, use one cup of water. Pour the mix into the water, stirring as you do. Now here comes the tricky bit. The plaster will actually begin to set the minute that the mix touches water. You have to stir this plaster for about four or five minutes until it has a pancake batter consistency.

Once your batter has reached the right consistency, tap the bottom of the bowl on the ground a few times and watch for air bubbles that will pop up through the batter. The less air bubbles, the better the track! Next, pour your material around the track; if you pour it into the track you may damage the print. I usually just follow the cardboard walls and pour an even layer around them. The plaster should fill in the track on it's own.

Let the dentist's stone set for its allotted time (usually about an hour). During your free time, you may want to wander and see if there are any other prints. During the drying process, the stone will turn a dull white, and after the hour of waiting, you should be able to tap on it and there should be no "give" to the material. If it is still a little doughy or has wet spots, let it dry some more. Humidity can be a factor and affect the drying time.

When it comes time to actually pick up the cast, you need to be very aware of how you do it. Crouch at one end of the mold and reach towards the other, get your fingers under the mold and pull towards you. Be very careful as your cast could still crack. Do not try to dust it off or anything else for several days. Do not pack it in plastic wrap; even though the plaster is dry, it still needs to let the leftover moisture escape. Paper is best the best way to store it, as it will wick the moisture away from the cast.

Be very careful when it comes time to clean your cast, especially if you are using plaster which can disintegrate when submerged in water. You don't need to be gentle with Dental stone; you can simply take a brush and clean it of dirt and debris. With the plaster, run it under gently running water in the sink; you'll want to clean the edges, but not the print itself, as this can actually sand away some of the details. Lightly brush it; do not try to get all of the dirt off. There will be some remaining;, that is normal.

Tips to Ensure a Great Cast

1. Once you start adding the mix to the water and stirring, you cannot add more water or more mix to change consistency. Do this before you start stirring. Otherwise, you can ruin the mixture altogether which will result in a weak, fragile cast.
2. Pay attention to expiration dates, as Plaster of Paris does have a shelf life. Using old plaster can result in very brittle and badly detailed casts.
3. Adding either vinegar (to slow down the setting of the cast) or salt (to speed it up) will change the makeup of the cast. This will result in making the casting softer than normal. If you need the plaster to harden up faster, and are not worried about the quality of the cast, use salt.
4. If you are casting a print in fine dry dust or sand, add more water to the mix. Making it a little more like liquid will allow you to save the details of the cast without destroying the print. Just give it a little more time to dry.
5. Use Snow Print Wax if you have to make a casting in snow. Pour the wax into the track; this will give you a nicely detailed base, next pour in your plaster. Please remember that the wax is, of course, wax and so it is soft and easy to scratch or damage; be very careful with it.
6. Paper towels and paper bags work fine to wrap your cast in; do not use newspaper, as it can stain your casting.
7. If the track is on a hill or slope, instead of using cardboard you can actually use the dirt or mud to create walls around the casting. Sometimes, it is difficult to get an even barrier using the cardboard when the land is uneven.
8. Do not use plaster to set a cast that is immersed in water or that has standing water in it, instead use dental stone and give it extra time to dry.
9. Wash all of your utensils and bowl in between castings (even if it is

five minutes later), as bits of hardened plaster or stone will remain on the equipment and then will contaminate your next batch. The incorporation of the old plaster with the new will result in a soft chalk-like casting that is very fragile.

10. When your cast has had several days to cure, you may paint it. Do not paint every surface and completely seal it. Moisture must still be allowed to escape the cast. It is best to paint only the details of the track.
11. Dental stone is a superior casting material. It is much harder than plaster, durable and gives better detail. Other types of gypsum cements include hydrostone, hydrocal, and die stone.
12. DO NOT use hobby plaster, modeling plaster, molding plaster, or patching cement for your bigfoot tracks.

Mothman

Shannon at the Mothman monument.

The Mothman is intriguing, with large red glowing eyes, piercing shriek voice, large wings, and standing around seven feet tall. It does sound like something from a science fiction movie, but it is just the opposite. There are some individuals who would swear this creature, known as the Mothman, was in fact real. Where did this creature originate from? Some of the locals in the town called Point Pleasant, located in West Virginia, have many stories and their own ideas and answers to this question. Some believe this creature is the murdered and tortured soul of a Shawnee leader who died in 1777, named Chief Cornstalk, coming back and taking revenge upon the town. That would not be the first time we have heard of such curses dwelling on the lips of locals from towns across the world. But there are many more theories on this creature, such as it came from chemicals that were once dumped by the local TNT plant, which in turn created a mutant-like creature. Or could it be some type of rare bird that made its way to Point Pleasant? We might not ever truly know that answer, but only what our imaginations allow.

Of course, there has been a theory that this being could be extraterrestrial in nature. But why then would the sightings last almost a year and then suddenly end after a traumatic event. On the night of December 15, 1967, the Silver Bridge, which connected West Virginia and Ohio via the Ohio River, suddenly collapsed, killing around forty-six people during rush-hour traffic.

What does this have to do with the Mothman? This creature's activity is said to have increased a short time prior to the Silver Bridge collapse. The event gained national and world headlines. But tales of the Mothman were not spoken in quiet whispers. Articles devoted to the idea of a winged insect-like creature sending out warnings days prior to the bridge falling eventually overshadowed the tragedy itself. Engineers believed the bridge was becoming weak in structure and it was only a matter of time before the bridge collapsed. Skeptics contend that it may have been a bit of mass hysteria, where a couple of people saw something and it was impactful enough to gain some attention. Soon enough, everyone was having "experiences."

After the bridge event had taken place, reports started coming into the local police department about strange lights being seen and unidentified flying objects around the Point Pleasant area. Were these flying objects there to take the Mothman back to where the creature originally came from? Today in the thriving town of Point Pleasant, the remains of the now-famous TNT plant still stands with endless underground tunnels and storage rooms. People come from all over for tours of the plant or perhaps in hopes to catch a glimpse of the famous creature.

New Jersey Devil

"It was three feet high... long black hair over its entire body, arms and hands like a monkey, face like a dog, split hooves and a tail a foot long."

~George Snyder
Moorestown, New Jersey
Sighting on January 20, 1909

The New Jersey Devil is a creature which through many legends told over time, has not changed that much. During the seventh century, supposedly, there was a woman who reached out to the devil and asked for another child. Some say the woman was rather loose with her female body, allowing any man to touch her in a sexual way. But sometimes legends tend to leave out most of the truth, and this could be the case with Mrs. Leeds, who also could have been (before marriage) a woman named Deborah Smith. Some individuals think that the woman's last name could have been Shroud and lived at Leeds Point. There seems to be some confusion as to who this woman truly was. But she was in fact just about to give birth to, yes, her thirteenth child; it was not uncommon during those times to have a large family. No other individuals state the location of the house where this child was born, but some would call it a "birthing house" and the local women would gather there to give birth to their children. During this time, the hysteria of witchcraft was still highly feared among the villagers. Could this have been the devil's child? Or a case of a deformity that, back in those times, people believed to be the effect of the family or child having been cursed by the devil?

The Leed family lived in an area called Pine Barrens, also known today as Leeds Point, and even over a few hundred years of time; reports of sightings of a creature with a head the shape of a horse, hoofs, and wings are still being seen and heard in the woods around that area.

Now if the mother did in fact have a disfigured child, then most likely the family kept the child inside and away from the local villagers. But what happened? Did the child escape from the home and become lost in the woods? Was the mother sick and then died; and if so, what about the rest of the family? How could a human being live that long, since the reports of the sightings date back so long ago? What about the hoof foot prints that have been found and the reports of a winged creature? Again in this field it is all about the evidence and research to seek the truth about such legends and creatures. Seems to be lots of questions without answers.

Another theory is that the creature is a form of a prehistoric creature that could have been living deep inside a cave or cavern, killing livestock and farmers crops, then hiding away from the human eye until it needed food again. Not sure about that theory, but one never knows because in the paranormal, sometimes stranger things have happened and have been discovered. Today, many come from all over to explore the remains of what was once a cabin in the woods, searching for a glimpse of what could be a demon, bird, or even a supernatural creature. Some parts of the areas involved are on private property, so please make sure to get the proper permission before exploring the woods.

Depiction of New Jersey Devil as appeared in a Philadelphia newspaper, 1909.

Chupacabra

This creature is widely known as the "blood sucker" for draining the blood from animals, especially farmers' livestock (such as goats). There have been reports of the attacks from Mexico to the United States and beyond into other countries, even including reports from Russia. These reports all seem to be close in the description of the creature – a dog-like animal with not much fur on the body and some backbone showing. Other reports have given the description of a hairless dog/rat-type of animal, sometimes with an overbite and a long tail. It has been reported that several types of this creature have been shot or trapped. Tests show, though, that the remains of the creatures to be coyotes and dogs suffering from a parasite infection and or a form of sarcoptic mange, which is a type of canine scabies. Cats, cattle, foxes, and most species of animals can get this; the animal becomes hairless for its entire life unless treated for the infection. Most likely, this animal, being in a sick state, could not hunt normally as a healthy animal could; that being said, perhaps it went on to weaker and smaller prey such as the goats, chickens, and other smaller livestock. The idea is not farfetched at all.

Still others feel this could be the work of a government experiment that went wrong or that somehow the creature escaped from the facility where it was being kept. Too, an animal could have been born a mutant due to the pollution and dump sites of nuclear waste or even waste from factories dumping into the rivers and other water sources. Again, this might not be too far from one of the truths, but does make one think and take a closer look at the facts.

What about the blood sucking? Why is it just taking the blood of the prey and not the whole animal? This does again raise some questions about the cattle that fall prey, but the cause of that seems to fall back to the theory of aliens. Yet the cattle's blood is drained and the only marks left behind appear like two fang or bite marks. Strange, indeed, and we are not suggesting the creature named Chupacabra is to blame, but it does make people scratch their heads on the subject when thinking of the similarities of the blood-sucking idea.

Coyotes with mange have been mistaken for chupacabra in the past.

Conclusion

Paranormal is a subject which will always bring intrigue, mystery, and skepticism to individuals. But the yearning for truth and evidence has exploded over time, each of us searching for answers about spirits, supernatural creatures, and even those intelligent life forms that may or may not dwell on other planets. Perhaps such proof has been right under our noses all along, but we as a society choose to not comprehend such truths. Evidence of such subjects will always become the center of controversy, but just like a so-called harmless rumor, there is always a form of truth twisted within it.

It's always best to keep the paranormal unwrapped!

Ghost Quest Paranormal Research Society
CLIENT INVESTIGATION FORM

DATE: [ ]

NAME:	
ADDRESS:	

CITY:		STATE:	ZIP CODE:
PHONE NO.:		CELL NO.:	
EMAIL:			

OWNERS/OCCUPANTS NAMES (INCLUDING YOURSELF)	GENDER (M / F)	RELATIONSHIP	DATE OF BIRTH / AGE

STRUCTURAL INFORMATION

BUILDING TYPE: (CHECK ONE)	Detached Residence ☐	Duplex ☐	Condo ☐	Apartment ☐	Other ☐

DO YOU OWN OR RENT?

NO. OF BEDROOMS:	BATHROOMS:	SQUARE FEET:	LOT SIZE (SQ. FT.):

ADDITIONAL ROOMS & OTHER INFORMATION:

HOW MANY YEARS AND/OR MONTHS HAVE YOU LIVED AT THE LOCATION?

Ghost Quest Paranormal Research Society
CLIENT INVESTIGATION FORM

ANY KNOWN HISTORY OF LOCATION? (STRUCTURAL CHANGES, PREVIOUS OCCUPANTS, OTHER PARANORMAL ACTIVITY, ETC.)

HAVE ANY OTHER BUILDINGS BEEN CONSTRUCTED ON THE SITE PREVIOUS TO THE CURRENT ONE? IF YES, EXPLAIN:

IS THERE ANY KNOWN HISTORY OF THE SURROUNDING AREA? (OLD SCHOOLS, GRAVE SITES, OLD COURTS, OLD CHURCHES, ETC.)

ARE THERE ANY ACCOUNTS OF PARANORMAL ACTIVITY AT YOUR PREVIOUS RESIDENCE?

WERE ANY TRAGEDIES OR DEATHS ASSOCIATED WITH THE IMMEDIATE AREA OR NEIGHBORHOOD? IF YES, EXPLAIN:

Ghost Quest Paranormal Research Society
CLIENT INVESTIGATION FORM

IS THERE ANY DOCUMENTATION OF PREVIOUS PARANORMAL ACTIVITY? (NEWSPAPER CLIPPINGS, ETC.)

RELIGIOUS & MEDICAL BACKGROUND

WHAT, IF ANY, IS YOUR RELIGIOUS BACKGROUND? (BOTH FAMILY AND YOUR PRESENT RELIGIOUS STATUS)

ANY HISTORY OF ALCOHOL OR DRUG ABUSE?

ANY HISTORY OF MENTAL ILLNESS? IF YES, EXPLAIN:

ANY HISTORY OF SERIOUS TRAUMA? (NEAR DEATH, RAPE, ETC.)

Ghost Quest Paranormal Research Society
CLIENT INVESTIGATION FORM

LIST ALL MEDICATIONS AND PRESCRIPTION ITEMS USED IN THE PAST THREE YEARS. INCLUDE ALL PRESCRIPTION DRUGS, OVER-THE-COUNTER DRUGS, PRESCRIPTION EYE GLASSES, CONTACT LENSES, ETC. PLEASE MAKE A SEPARATE LIST FOR EACH OCCUPANT.

HAVE ANYONE'S PRESCRIPTIONS CHANGED RECENTLY?

ANY OTHER FAMILY HISTORY YOU THINK IS IMPORTANT?

WHEN DID THE CURRENT DISTURBANCES BEGIN AND WHAT HAPPENED FIRST?

WHAT DID YOU THINK OF THESE DISTURBANCES?

4

Ghost Quest Paranormal Research Society
CLIENT INVESTIGATION FORM

HAVE YOU LOOKED FOR ORDINARY, NORMAL EXPLANATIONS? WHAT MAKES YOU THINK IT'S PARANORMAL?

WHEN DID THE MOST RECENT INCIDENT OCCUR AND WHAT HAPPENED?

HAVE THE DISTURBANCES BEEN INCREASING IN FREQUENCY AND/OR SEVERITY SINCE THEY FIRST BEGAN?

ARE EVENTS MORE FREQUENT AT CERTAIN TIMES DURING THE 24 HOURS OF THE DAY THAN AT OTHERS? IF YES, WHAT TIMES?

IS THERE A PATTERN OF ANY KIND TO THESE DISTURBANCES THAT YOU'VE NOTICED (FOR EXAMPLE, WHEN THE EVENTS OCCURRED, WHAT SORTS OF OBJECTS WERE AFFECTED, WHAT LOCATIONS WERE INVOLVED, WHO WAS AROUND AT THE TIME, ETC.)?

IS ACTIVITY MORE FREQUENT IN CERTAIN PLACES (FOR EXAMPLE, IN CERTAIN ROOMS OF THE HOUSE) THAN IN OTHERS? IF YES, WHERE?

Ghost Quest Paranormal Research Society
CLIENT INVESTIGATION FORM

DO THE OCCURRENCES HAPPEN MORE FREQUENTLY IN THE PRESENCE OR VICINITY OF CERTAIN PERSONS THAN THEY DO WITH OTHERS? IF YES, STATE WHICH PEOPLE. ALSO, DO THE EVENTS TAKE PLACE WHEN THEY ARE NOT IN THE AREA?

HAVE THERE BEEN ANY WITNESSES FROM OUTSIDE THE HOUSEHOLD? WHAT DID THEY EXPERIENCE, AS FAR AS YOU KNOW?

HAS ANYONE EVER SEEN AN OBJECT START TO MOVE WHEN NO ONE WAS NEAR IT? IF YES, DESCRIBE ALL SUCH OCCURRENCES.

IF THERE HAVE BEEN UNEXPLAINED MOVEMENTS OF OBJECTS, WAS THERE ANYTHING STRANGE ABOUT THE MANNER IN WHICH THE OBJECTS MOVED OR STOPPED? (E.G.: OBJECTS THAT MOVE AROUND CORNERS, OR HIT WITH UNUSUALLY GREAT FORCE, ETC.)

HAVE YOU OR ANYONE IN THE RESIDENCE EVER USED OR EXPERIMENTED WITH OUIJI BOARDS, SÉANCES, ETC.?

Ghost Quest Paranormal Research Society
CLIENT INVESTIGATION FORM

HAVE YOU OR ANYONE IN THE RESIDENCE EVER USED OR EXPERIMENTED WITH BLACK MAGIC OR USED ANY TYPE OF WITCHCRAFT FOR PERSONAL GAIN? (E.G.: MONEY, LOVE, FAME, ETC.) IF YES, PLEASE EXPLAIN:

HOW WOULD YOU LIKE TO BE HELPED?

Ghost Quest Paranormal Research Society
CLIENT INVESTIGATION FORM

HAVE ANY OF THE OCCUPANTS ENCOUNTERED ANY OF THE FOLLOWING? (EXPLAIN ALL THAT APPLY)

1. Voices:
2. Smells/Odors:
3. Shadows:
4. Orbs:
5. Smoky Forms:
6. Strong Random Thoughts:
7. Strong Feelings/Emotions:
8. Cold Spots:
9. Hot Spots:
10. Recent Death of Loved One:
11. Recent Anniversary of Loved One's Death, Birthday, Anniversary, etc.:
12. Sounds (Walking, Running, Knocking, etc.):
13. Door(s) Opening/Closing:
14. Mood Changes, Especially in One Room:
15. Conversations With Spirits:
16. Conversations Between Spirits:
17. Disappearing Objects:
18. Objects Moving:

8

Ghost Quest Paranormal Research Society
CLIENT INVESTIGATION FORM

19. Puberty of Family Member or Emotional Stress of Adolescents in Area: ☐

20. Renovations to Location: ☐

21. Electrical Disturbances (Frequent Light Bulb Burnouts, etc.): ☐

22. Problems with Appliances (TV, Radio, Stereo, Computers, Clocks, Microwave, etc.): ☐

23. Headaches or Dizziness: ☐

24. Feeling of Being Touched: ☐

25. Physical Harm (Scratches, Cuts, Bites, etc.): ☐

Ghost Quest Paranormal Research Society
CLIENT INVESTIGATION FORM

ANY ADDITIONAL INFORMATION, NOTES OR QUESTIONS

BIBLIOGRAPHY

http://www.uspto.gov/trademarks/basics/definitions.jsp. "Trademarks Process – Trademark, Patent or Copyright?" Dec.13, 2011.

http://www.invention-protection.com "Trademarks – Understanding the Principle & the Supplemental Register" Gallagher & Dawsey Co., LPA. April 2010.

http://www.uspto.gov/trademarks/process/index.jsp "Trademark Process" July 07, 2009.

Miles, Kathleen. "UC Riverside To Study Afterlife With $5 Million Grant For 'The Immortality Project'" Huffington Post (Online), Aug.02,2012. http://www.huffingtonpost.com/2012/08/02/uc-riverside-afterlife-the-immortality-project_n_1734603.html

Manch, David J. "A Theory on the Origins of UFOs." Interview 2012.

RESOURCES

Here are some great sites which we encourage everyone to check out.

Official Sites:

Shannon Sylvia's Official Site: www.shannonsylvia.com
Katie Boyd's Official Site: www.katieboyd.net

Informational Sites:

Trademark and Copyright information: http://www.uspto.gov

Extraterrestrial Informational Sites:

www.daniken.com
www.hyper.net/ufo/occupants.html
www.legendarytimes.com
www.mufon.com
www.roswellufomuseum.com
www.ufoabduction.com/faq1.htm

Supernatural Creatures

http://bigfootcountry.net
http://www.bigfootmuseum.com
www.newanimal.org/links.htm
www.njdevilhunters.com/hunts.html
www.pinelandsalliance.org

Other Cool Sites:

www.beyondghosts.com
http://ghoststop.com
http://nyackparanormal.com
www.beckahthepsychic.com
www.ghostquest.org
www.hauntednevada.com
www.pararocktv.com
www.tenacityradio.com
www.theharleyhouse.com
www.spiritsofnewengland.org
www.stevenalachance.com

NOTES: